Law and Education Inequality

Removing Barriers to Educational Opportunities

A volume in
Law and Education
Susan C. Bon and Jeffrey C. Sun, *Series Editors*

Law and Education Inequality

Removing Barriers to Educational Opportunities

edited by

Susan C. Bon
University of South Carolina

Jeffrey C. Sun
University of Louisville

IAP

INFORMATION AGE PUBLISHING, INC.
Charlotte, NC • www.infoagepub.com

Library of Congress Cataloging-in-Publication Data

A CIP record for this book is available from the Library of Congress
http://www.loc.gov

ISBN: 978-1-68123-173-0 (Paperback)
978-1-68123-174-7 (Hardcover)
978-1-68123-175-4 (ebook)

Printed and bound by CPI Group (UK) Ltd, Croydon, CR0 4YY

CONTENTS

for change, the literature is bereft of analyses that couple a critical legal lens that is infused with social science research as a way to draw an innovative, prosocial response.

The purpose of this book is to examine the role of law as potentially countering or impeding desirable education reforms, but it calls on readers to consider how policymakers, lawyers, social scientists, and educators might best alter the course or accept the conditions in an effort to advance a more just and less unequal educational system. This book accomplishes that purpose by posing problems about legislation, regulations, and judicial decisions that present barriers to achieving education equality. Then it offers policy solutions that advance educational standards, priorities, and practices.

In presenting the topics of law and educational inequality, we divided the book into five parts. Part I explores the role of schools as organizations and their governance structures to uncover the educational inequalities emergent among charter school operations.

As an alternative educational organization to traditional public schools, charter schools have come under scrutiny because their organizational design draws on local resources but typically affords independence or high degrees of autonomy from the state and/or the local school district. Such corporate autonomy derives from the school charter or legislative contract with the jurisdiction, and that relationship has spurred questions of an undemocratic form of educational privilege for middle- to upper-class families with resources and time to establish these schools.

The charter school movement is not insignificant. Charter schools have increased in number and share of public schools. Between the 1999–2000 and 2011–2012 school years, the number of public charter schools increased from 1,500 to 5,700 (U.S. Department of Education, 2014a). Those numbers equate to growth of 380% in 12 years. Although the actual percentage share of public charter schools remains relatively small at 5.8% as of the 2011–2012 school year, the number of students increased from 0.3 million to 2.1 million students within that same time frame. Thus, the charter school movement cannot be overlooked in a discussion about education law and inequality.

In Chapter 1, Daniel Kiel raises the educational reform paradox in which the solution to the education equity rhetoric is differentiated school choice. Kiel describes how some local districts are now opting for the portfolio model, which presents multiple operators functioning within a community. The differentiated schools within a common education community allow student choice of schools from traditional public schools in the district, charter schools led by a charter management organization, charter schools led by an independent charter operator, and a school taken over by the state (or under state receivership). Kiel raises the question, Can a model built upon differentiation and choice drive more equitable education opportunities? In aiding the discussion, he presents the intuition and assumptions of schools and how educational lawyers, policymakers, and leaders must reimagine schools under a portfolio model to understand how they might succeed. He also offers guidance to lawyers, social science researchers, policymakers, school operators, and parents/caregivers on how to proceed with evaluating and responding to potential barriers.

In Chapter 2, Charles Russo and Gerald Cattaro build on the discussion of educational inequality by examining the constitutional permissibility of faith-based charter schools. As the authors aptly note, "Faith-based charter schools are seeking to fill the void left by the closing of religiously affiliated nonpublic schools," yet a review of key cases suggest that laws creating faith-based charter schools would likely withstand federal and, in many instances, state constitutions. The authors are unfettered by this legal likelihood. Russo and Cattaro recognize the value of distancing faith-based schools from governmental oversight and intervention.

In Part II, Chapters 3 and 4 address legal and policy efforts aimed at supporting English Language Learners (ELLs). This issue is of particular interest as the population of ELL students has steadily grown, particularly in 23 states that have shown gains of more than 6% between the 2002–2003 and 2011–2012 academic years alone (U.S. Department of Education, 2014b). Further, recent executive actions by President Barak Obama have included the Deferred Action for Childhood Arrivals (DACA). DACA is a form of prosecutorial discretion; it defers actions to qualified individuals from removal proceedings for a specified time and allows approved individuals to remain in the United States for multiple purposes including to seek an education.

English Language Learners have faced many barriers to receiving a quality education that leads to supporting student achievement. In Chapter 3, Carrie Sampson and Sonya Horsford examine ELL funding for 10 states experiencing the largest ELL population growth within a ten-year period. Their analysis highlights the variability in funding amounts and programming for ELL students. They argue that ELL funding is positively correlated with higher student achievement, and reframe the narrative around ELL funding support as an investment, not a burdensome expense.

In Chapter 4, Philip T. K. Daniel and Jeffrey Sun also identify funding as a significant barrier to student achievement; however, they offer a different solution to resolving the inequities. Specifically, Daniel and Sun propose an integration of resources among schools, universities, and governmental agencies. They call their approach the School-University-Policy Practice Model (SUPP Model).

Their SUPP Model adopts a triple-helix metaphor. This metaphor is common in looking at how educational entities, industry, and government may collaborate for research commercialization efforts. Thus, much like

Sampson's approach, the focus is on framing the solution as a resource investment.

In addition to ELL students, students with disabilities are often at the center of the educational inequality dialogue. In Part III, we present Chapters 5 and 6, which each tackle the overlooked analyses of student transitions to new educational environments. Specifically, in Chapter 5, Brenda Kallio, Richard Geisel, and Angela Jonasson present legal and administrative responses to life-threatening allergies as a child with disabilities transitions from home to school. Their chapter explains the applicability of legal protections such as Americans with Disabilities Act, Section 504 of the Rehabilitation Act, Food Allergy and Anaphylaxis Act, and state laws on self-carry or self-administer laws permitting emergency medication carrying and self-administering. Kallio, Geisel, and Jonasson also offer guidance on protection rights for the students' educational and medical records to clarify privacy and institutional access.

In Chapter 6, Susan Bon and Nicole Snyder move the discussion of student transitions from the P–12 educational setting to the postsecondary environments such as training, education, and employment. Bon and Snyder identify key barriers to student supports for transition plans. One clear problem is the lack of accountability, which is typically drawn from enforceable provisions under the law. For instance, while the absence of a transition plan marks an error in a student's Individualized Education Program (IEP), the omission does not arise to procedural error or the denial of a free appropriate public education, pursuant to the Individuals with Disabilities Act. Another problem, which has been repeatedly described in the literature as a substantial barrier to student success, is the service cliff provided between the P–12 educational environment and postsecondary educational institutions. Given the barriers of the poor accountability and the service cliff, Bon and Snyder propose several intervening actions that would mediate some of the transition problems. Most notably, Bon and Snyder suggest a transition plan that develops students with disabilities appropriately by adopting evidence-based practices such as self-determination skills. The authors recognize the need for building individual programs that develop self-initiated actions toward greater independence.

Part III continues the discussion of educational inequality through social marginalization through student-on-student bullying. Chapters 7 and 8 follow the common thread of addressing students' exercising of social and physical power and the legal and policy responses to combat these harmful behaviors. Richard Geisel, Brenda Kallio, and Christa Brodina present in Chapter 7 various legal claims possible to assert based on bullying behavior. As they indicate, federal laws draw on protections for special classes of individuals such as discrimination based on race, color, national origin, sex, and disability. Thus, the application of the law is potentially limiting. By contrast, states with antibullying laws tend to have broader coverage of impermissible behavior, yet Geisel, Kallio, and Brodina have uncovered great variability among what the laws require for schools to do in order to address bulling behavior. The authors compared each state's legislation to the Dear Colleague letter jointly authored by the U.S. Departments of Health and Human Services and Education. The Dear Colleague letter established a set of guidelines based on research and practice, and this chapter highlights the gap between statutory requirements and informed research and practice.

In Chapter 8, Christine Bellini and Julian Kitchen evaluate the effectiveness of laws and policies and their effect on school climate for lesbian, gay, bisexual, and transgender (LGBT) students. The authors surveyed Gay-Straight Alliances advisors to investigate these effects and found that laws and policies advancing inclusion along with grassroots student-led activities improve the educational environment for LGBT students. Thus, while laws and policies play an instrumental role, bottom-up initiatives also have a significant impact on culture change for LGBT students and contribute to the educational equality and antibullying/harassment behaviors.

Part IV rounds off the book by exploring the extent of courts' deferential treatment to colleges in determining teacher candidate qualifications. Both Chapters 9 and 10 examine that issue through case law contesting a college's evaluation of a teacher candidate's disposition (i.e., beliefs, attitudes, and values) consistent with the educational mission. In Chapter 9, Lawrence Kajs, Betty Grigsby, and Kent Divoll examine recent case law in this area and conclude that courts have generally deferred to the academic institution based on the college faculty's professional judgments. To help avoid litigation and clarify the standards, Kajs, Grigsby, and Divoll outline recommended policies and procedures that help maintain fairness and clear communication of the standards.

Similarly, in Chapter 10, Thomas Sheeran, Vincent Rinaldo, Michael Smith, and Walter Polka find that courts tend to defer to professional judgments of academics in more defined areas such as grading, program acceptance, and program continuation. Yet the authors question the judicial consistency with granting deference on the more "intangible" evaluations of teacher candidates who are enrolled in a college's teacher education program. They suggest that field develop is a more defensible evaluation system or instrument, much like assessments in other professional fields such as law, medicine, dentistry, and pharmacy.

Our intent with this book was not to present an exhaustive list of issues or to introduce basic concepts in education law. Instead, we sought to spur the dialogue on key topics challenging the field. In addition, we sought to expand the lens beyond the study of law. This book addresses educational inequality using a transdisciplinary lens. It is our belief that these topics

ACKNOWLEDGMENTS

This Information Age Publishing (IAP) series reflects the collective efforts and passions of many scholars and practitioners who focus on law and education. We appreciate the support and encouragement from George Johnson, who approached us with the idea of embarking on this project, and Brittany Black, who supported us through the publication process. As with any new project, the idea developed and evolved slowly over time, but gained momentum as authors began submitting their work for consideration.

This book is the second in the Law & Education series, and is focused on efforts to address law and educational inequality, particularly in terms of removing barriers of race, class, gender, and/or disability. The book, titled *Law & Education Inequality: Removing Barriers to Educational Opportunities*, would not have come together without the thoughtful contributions and numerous brainstorming sessions with respected education law colleagues Dr. Kevin Brady of North Carolina State University and Dr. Karen Miksch of the University of Minnesota. In addition, we would like to acknowledge the many reviewers, doctoral students, and recent doctoral graduates who contributed their time and talent during the editorial process. The following individuals, in particular, made this book project possible by providing their expert feedback and thoughtful reviews of the submitted chapters:

David Buckman, PhD, Instructor at the University of South Carolina, Columbia, SC;

Stefania D. Petcu, PhD, Administrative Assistant, National Resource Center for the First-Year Experience and Students in Transition, Columbia, SC;

Law and Education Inequality, pages xv–xvi

Delia E. Racines, PhD, Faculty, Rossier School of Education, University of Southern California, Los Angeles, CA.

Karen A. Schade, CEO/Principal, School Lane Charter School, Bensalem, PA 19020

PART I

ORGANIZATION AND GOVERNANCE

premised on the assumption that today's schools can be improved and educational opportunity can be made considerably more equitable through a system of schools that are meaningfully different from one another (Hill & Campbell, 2011).

As the momentum and popularity of school choice policies have increased, a radically new structure based on this quest for difference is emerging (Minow, 2011). The most fundamental change within local communities embracing the school choice structure is in who has the authority to operate schools. In place of a single school district serving everyone is a system of autonomous school operators serving a common localized community (Hill & Campbell, 2011). Students and families can not only choose among schools with different specialties, such as the arts or engineering, but also among schools operated by wholly different entities.

The local communities embracing this change in structure, often referred to as the "portfolio model," are generally metropolitan, urban areas with significant minority and economically disadvantaged student populations. Despite social and economic disparities, these communities embrace this structural shift in a variety of ways. New Orleans, for example, relies heavily on charter schools to serve the city's student population, and in Memphis, the traditional public school district will continue to serve the majority of students alongside a growing state and charter presence (Kiel, 2013).

The paradox of the use of school choice to achieve educational equity or fairness is that schools are deliberately designed to be different from one another and, in a sense, unequal. Different schools run by different operators can use different methods and pedagogical approaches to serve their students. This autonomy is granted with the hope that it will lead to improved educational opportunities for all students. Whether such differentiation can successfully increase equity in educational opportunities should be the central question for the portfolio model.

While the structure varies from place to place depending upon circumstances, such as funding and student population size, the portfolio model rests upon three common and foundational principles. First, to ensure genuine choice in educational offerings, the model embraces the idea of a diverse group of school operators serving a single community competing for students. Second, to ensure flexibility and innovation, the model grants significant autonomy to school operators to function independently of one another. Finally, to ensure accountability for these autonomous operators, the model makes the operator's continued authority to run schools contingent upon their demonstrated record of success. This chapter will use the term "portfolio model" to refer to any system of public education that has embraced these principles, while acknowledging that particulars will vary.

Policymakers present shifting to the portfolio model as a mechanism for addressing persistent disparities in educational opportunity across lines of race and income in local communities (Hill et al., 2009). However, in order for policy shift to impact disparities and not merely be a change in structure, education advocates and policy analysts must be fully aware of the various policy implications of redistributing control of public education to address the inherent risks involved in doing so. Whether it be educators working within this new structure, researchers developing policy questions to address efficacy, or lawyers working to ensure legal compliance, a firm grasp of a portfolio model and the most significant barriers to success is essential. This chapter seeks to describe the emerging portfolio model structure along with some of the leading sources of its development and present the major practical, legal, and political ramifications of its adoption.

The Portfolio Model

In addition to altering the traditional structure of public education, the portfolio model also radically changes the jargon commonly used in public education. Since the transition to a portfolio model impacts the meaning of a common public school district, this chapter will use "district" or "traditional district" to refer to the familiar structure where schools report to a common school board and superintendent. Though districts will continue to exist in a portfolio model, they will no longer be the sole entity running schools within an area. Thus, where "district" may have once encompassed all of the schools within geographic boundaries, that definition is no longer appropriate in a portfolio model. When referring to all the schools in an area, this chapter will use the term "educational community."

In addition, the portfolio model rests upon the presence of multiple operators and potentially multiple authorizers. "Operator" will refer to any entity running a school, while "authorizer" will refer to entities, such as a district or the state, which grants operators their authority to run a school.

Multiple Operators

The portfolio model substantially alters the answer to the question, Who is in charge of local public education? Whereas a traditional district managed by a superintendent and governed by a school board have ultimate authority for all public education in a community, that power is dispersed among multiple operators within the portfolio model. While the traditional school district typically still exists as a school operator, it serves substantially fewer students and has little to no authority over other operators.

The most autonomous operator in the model is the state, typically in the form of a state-level school district created to takeover schools performing poorly. The most developed example of this type of entity is the Recovery School District (RSD) in Louisiana, which took over the bulk of public education in New Orleans following Hurricane Katrina in 2005. Emulating the RSD model, a number of states created similar districts, given authority under state law to take over struggling schools (Oluwole & Green, 2009; Saiger, 2006).

The growing presence of charter schools represents another type of autonomous school operator. Charter schools are often operated by private boards and administrators, but are funded with public money and are tuition free. A charter operator obtains its authority to run a school on the basis of a contract, or charter, with an authorizer, and is governed by state charter school laws. Historically, charter schools received their operational authority from local school districts, but an increasing number of states allow authorization at the state level as well (NACSA, 2012). Some charter schools are run by independent charter school operators, while others are part of larger networks of schools run by a common charter management organization. Thus, charter schools within a community may be authorized by either the local district or the state and may exist as single schools or as parts of larger networks.

In addition to RSD and charter schools, publicly supported virtual schools are now able to draw their student populations from throughout the state. In some states, publicly funded voucher systems make private schools accessible to a broader educational community (Louisiana Revised Statutes Annotated, 2013; Tennessee Code Annotated, 2013).

The presence of multiple operators in a school choice system provides a structure that enables the second foundational principle—autonomy—to be genuine. In the absence of a centralized traditional district setting policy for the entire community, schools run by the diverse group of operators are given the freedom to develop their own policies and practices. For example, independent operators may have the ability to alter the length of the school day or the school year or to develop a specialized curriculum. Perhaps the most significant autonomy is the freedom for each operator to make its own hiring and staffing decisions. State takeover districts and charter schools are explicitly granted this type of flexibility. In addition, schools within the traditional district may also be granted the autonomy to differentiate their educational program. In Chicago, for example, district schools that demonstrate significant student academic improvement can apply for autonomy from district rules and programs without their operation being shifted to an independent operator (Sartain et al., 2009).

Proponents of the portfolio model often highlight autonomy as a necessary component for allowing the innovation required to improve education (Hill et al., 2009). Figure 3.1 depicts one potential version of a portfolio model, with its various operators and authorizers serving a common educational community. Without the flexibility of autonomy, schools would be unable to test new methods of instruction or differing programs targeted at

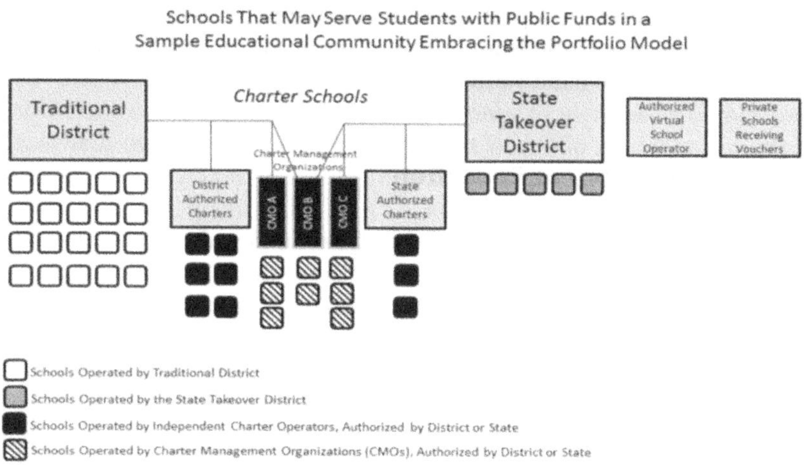

Figure 3.1 Operator Autonomy.

serving students with diverse needs. Whereas the traditional district might have been slow to implement innovative programs, independent operators would have the ability to do so more easily and without concern about any impact on other schools.

Hyperaccountability

In exchange for broad autonomy, independent school operators in a portfolio model have their very existence at stake based upon how well they deliver for their students. Although the past two decades have seen increasingly rigorous systems of accountability applied to struggling schools and districts, the portfolio model relies upon a high-stakes accountability system for all operators. Operators who do not achieve articulated goals will lose their authority to run schools, while those who perform well may be granted expanded authority or autonomy or both.

Under the traditional district model, the district's continued authority to operate schools could be taken for granted—the district existed, had always existed, and would continue to exist. However, within a portfolio model, an operator's authority, including that of the traditional district, is constantly under evaluation and could be terminated if results dictate.

In addition to this formal system of accountability, the fact that schools in the portfolio model compete for a common pool of students provides an additional accountability lever. Since school funding depends upon student enrollment, schools that develop a reputation for failure will, if the market

limited to oversight or charter approval and for some schools, such as those operated by state takeover districts, the local board, and, by extension, the voters who elect it, will have no authority whatsoever.

In place of democratic accountability, a portfolio model provides more narrow but more severe school-level accountability. The school operator is thus held accountable by those with which it has the closest relationship—its authorizer and its students—rather than by the entire community. Families dissatisfied with an operator's performance can simply enroll elsewhere in a multi-operator system. Authorizers dissatisfied with an operator's performance will have the ability to revoke the operator's authority, a process that is governed both by statute and by whatever contract exists between the authorizer and operator.

This change redefines what is meant by "public" when discussing public education. For a private operator governed by its own board, responsible for hiring its own staff, and given the flexibility to run a school its own way, the only thing that is public about the school is financial—it receives public funding and attendance is free. This, of course, is significant and may be the essence of what makes a school a public school, but it is substantially different from a district of common schools shared by a community.

Practical

The shift to a portfolio model not only affects the idea of public education, it affects how public education functions as well. Through much of the 20th century, traditional public education was marked by a process of centralization, with smaller districts consolidating for reasons of efficiency (Berry, 2006). Centralization is so attractive to policymakers because it allows districts more robust purchasing power as well as the flexibility to easily distribute resources where they are needed. The portfolio model cuts against both of these advantages and is likely to be more expensive than a traditional district.

Although they generally have greater autonomy, independent school operators still must spend money on similar expenses. Compared to a traditional district where spending for food-related expenses can come from an operating budget generated for the entire district, in a portfolio model, each independent operator is responsible for finding its own vendor and negotiating its own contract. Thus, instead of a single food contract, the fact of multiple operators should lead to a multiplicity of food contracts.

Similarly, traditional districts not only centralize funding but also expertise. For students with disabilities, for instance, the district office is able to develop a plan to serve students across many schools. In a portfolio model, however, the same bifurcation as is found with food-related expenses is more likely to develop with special-education services—each operator must develop its own plan.

Food and special-education services are only two of numerous examples where the shift to multiple operators acting independently is more likely to lead to a duplication of effort, with the negative impact of increasing overall costs. The multiple operators are no longer able to draw upon the pooling of both tangible resources and intangible expertise that can allow for more efficient spending and more effective practices. This raises important policy questions both for schools run by new operators as well as those that continue to be run by the traditional district. For new operators, will they be able to provide the level of service necessary to meet students' needs with the money they are given? For traditional districts, what will be the impact of the loss of students and funds on the schools and students that continue to be served by the district?

Given this inherent complexity as well as the high costs of starting up a new school, many new operators have relied heavily upon public and private grants to fill the financial gap (Cowen Institute, 2012). Since such money is not guaranteed, this reliance on "soft" money raises additional questions about the financial sustainability of a model that, according to its own terms, will require time to allow innovative and successful operators to flourish and struggling operators to disappear.

Finally, the shift to a portfolio model often allows for less flexibility in responding to changes in a local community's education needs. When a traditional district sees changes in where students live or in what services a particular school needs, it is able to shift its own resources to meet such needs. In the portfolio model, however, the fact that each operator is responsible only for its own students inhibits both the ability to see the broader picture and, to the extent such a picture can be seen, the ability to adapt to meet changes.

Legal

The philosophical and practical effects of moving to the portfolio model also produce legal concerns. As an initial matter, the multitude of laws that have been written to govern a model of public education based upon a traditional district may no longer be suitable. Crucial areas, such as school funding, student assignment, and schemes of accountability operate on the premise of a local system as the primary point of contact. The shift to a portfolio model will more likely require adjustments to such laws to reflect the fact of multiple, autonomous operators.

In addition, there have been legal challenges based upon the philosophical and practical effects of decentralization, and more suits are likely as the portfolio model is embraced elsewhere. For example, there have been challenges to the constitutionality of delegating operating authority to charter school operators (League of Women Voters of Washington, 2013). Of greater importance are charges that some operators, specifically charter schools, are not complying with special education laws. In New Orleans, for example, a class-action legal challenge along these lines has threatened the viability of that community's portfolio model (Garda, 2012; GAO, 2012).

THE CRUCIAL QUESTION: DOES THE PORTFOLIO MODEL DRIVE EQUITY?

Thus, even though the move toward portfolio models has enjoyed political support from both parties and at both the state and national level, the effects of such a shift make its long-term viability anything but certain. The future momentum of the model will depend in part on how these issues are resolved, but should also hinge upon how successful the model is at eliminating barriers to educational opportunities. After all, redefining the meaning of "public" education, spending more taxpayer dollars, and wading into potential legal issues should only be done if the model can solve the problem it has set out to address. Can a model built upon differentiation and choice drive more equitable educational opportunities?

The history of American public education demonstrates that where less successful schools exist within a community, it is more likely to be poor or minority students assigned to them. Historically, school choice has exacerbated this problem. In the 1960s, freedom-of-choice plans were utilized to slow the pace of desegregation until the Supreme Court intervened (Green v. County School Board of New Kent County, 1968). Later, magnet schools often had student populations that were disproportionately White and wealthy compared to surrounding communities, raising charges of a return to separate, unequal schooling (Minow, 2011; Ryan, 2010). Further, choice has been utilized by many families to avoid enrollment in urban school systems altogether, either through enrollment in private schools or by moving beyond district boundaries to attend suburban school districts. The result of many of these choices has been many urban schools that are socioeconomically and racially isolated, serving students who do not have the opportunity—through academic qualification, parental involvement or resources, or geographic location—to attend a community's higher-quality schools.

A portfolio model that replicates this situation would be a failure. While portfolio advocates suggest the model could increase educational opportunities, the decentralized model itself may actually increase the risk of stratification. The separation of students into groups served by independent operators could turn charges of separate, unequal schooling into fact—students *would* be served by separate operators; those operators could be delivering different, and unequal, educational opportunities; and all of this would be legally permissible.

There are three primary reasons that this could be the way a portfolio model develops in spite of the claims of its advocates. First, student choice could be restrained by either legal or practical limitations, thus removing some of an operator's incentive to deliver higher-quality education. Second, the competitive nature of a system of school choice would tend to work against the sharing of resources and best practices and the type of comprehensive planning necessary to create a stable and equitable system of schools. Finally, reluctance on the part of authorizers to remove operational authority from unsuccessful operators could negate the process of rewarding successful operators and eliminating unsuccessful ones.

Broad choice is essential to the theory of the portfolio model as it serves as the mechanism through which families and students can hold schools accountable. However, choices can be constrained in a variety of ways. Families may lack knowledge about a school, its program, and its quality, and they may be discouraged from enrolling either directly by operators seeking a certain type of student or indirectly by an opaque application process. Local school assignment policies may create default assignments to schools, such as geographic-based assignments, which leave few seats available for other students to choose. Or families may be unable to exercise choices due to practical constraints, such as a lack of transportation. As a result, not every school will be accessible to every student, diminishing the choices families have as well as the pressure on schools to compete in order to draw families to enroll.

Although access is crucial, so too is quality. Increasing the number of high-quality schools could be achieved through mechanisms to improve less successful schools and, where necessary, eliminate such schools from the pool of choices. It is not clear that the portfolio model will do either without deliberate effort.

The competitive nature of a portfolio district is held by advocates as a driver of innovation that could improve less successful schools. However, because operators are competing for students, the structure of a portfolio model makes it *less* likely that operators would share best practices with one another and makes it more likely that unsuccessful schools will continue to struggle.

In addition, competition could decrease the chance that operators would work together to minimize the inefficiencies inherent in the portfolio model. Indeed, the relationship between charter operators and traditional districts has not been productive in most places. A side effect of this discord is an inability for operators within portfolio models to work cohesively to serve a broader community. Combined with the lack of access and the fact

tive school placement. This includes ensuring that unsuccessful operators lose operational authority.

School Operators (Districts, Charter Schools, and State Personnel)

- School operators must be willing to cooperate with one another and resist the impulse to merely compete with other operators within a local community. This includes being willing to pool tangible resources to obtain financial efficiency and share operational expertise to ensure higher-quality education throughout the community.

Parents and Caregivers

- In a system of choice, the onus for choosing the best school rests with the student's family. Parents and caregivers must stay informed regarding school options, as well as the choice and application process.
- Similarly, parents and caregivers must be willing to exercise their level of accountability within a portfolio model—the ability to exit an unsuccessful school. Failure to do so reduces the incentives for unsuccessful operators to improve and for authorizers to terminate the authority of such operators to run schools.

The movement to disperse authority for public education to a multitude of operators should not mean that no one is considering the overall picture of education within a community. Policymakers, parents, and school operators should work to create a local entity tasked with filling this need. Such an entity may be governmental or nonprofit, but must be independent of all operators. Its duties should include facilitating the sharing of best practices, providing accurate information to the community, and keeping track of community needs in order to advise policymakers on methods to address them. Ultimately, this entity could return a sense of common purpose to a community's schools, even as they are run by autonomous operators.

The idea of making schooling more equal by making it more different is a paradox. Managing a portfolio model so that it moves a community toward educational equity will be a challenge. However, as efforts to standardize education have yet to eliminate disparities along lines of race and poverty, the portfolio model represents a radically different solution. Its success or failure in this regard will depend upon laws and policies that are intentional about making the most of this emerging structure.

NOTE

1. The Institute on Race and Poverty is now the Institute on Metropolitan Opportunity.

REFERENCES

Berry, C. (2006, May). School consolidation and inequality. *Brookings Papers on Education Policy, 2006/2007,* (9), 49–75. Retrieved from http://www.brookings.edu/gs/brown/bpepconference/Berry_paper.pdf

Cowen Institute on Public Education Initiatives. (2012). *The 2012 state of public education in New Orleans.* New Orleans, LA: Tulane University.

Garda, R. (2012). Culture class: Special education in charter schools. *North Carolina Law Review, 90,* 655–722.

Green v. County Sch. Bd. of New Kent Cnty., 391 U.S. 430 (1968).

Hill, P., & Campbell, C. (2011). *Portfolio school districts: Strife and progress in transforming public education in big cities.* Seattle, WA: Center on Reinventing Public Education.

Hill, P., Campbell, C., Menefee-Libey, D., Dusseault, B., DeArmond, M., & Gross, B. (2009). *Portfolio school districts for big cities: An interim report.* Seattle, WA: Center on Reinventing Public Education.

Institute on Race and Poverty.1 (2010). *The state of public schools in post-Katrina New Orleans: The challenge of creating equal opportunity.* Bloomington: University of Minnesota.

Kiel, D. (2013). The endangered school district: The promise and challenge of redistributing control of public education. *Boston University Public Interest Law Journal, 22*(2), 341–404.

League of Women Voters of Washington v. State, Case No. 13-2-24977-4 (Superior Court of King County, Wa., 2013).

Louisiana Revised Statutes Annotated §17:4011 (2013).

Minow, M. (2011). Confronting the seduction of school choice: Law, education and American pluralism. *Yale Law Journal, 120,* 814–848.

National Association of Charter School Authorizers (NACSA). (2012). *The state of charter school authorizing 2012.* Retrieved from http://www.qualitycharters.org/assets/files/Documents/Publications/2012%20Facts%20Report.pdf

Oluwole, J. O., & Green, P. C., III (2009). State takeovers of school districts: Race and the equal protection clause. *Indiana Law Review, 42,* 343–655.

Ravitch, D. (2012, March 6). Bobby Jindal v. public education. *Education Week Blog: Bridging Differences.* Retrieved from http://blogs.edweek.org/edweek/Bridging-Differences/2012/03/bobby_jindal_vs_public_educati.html

Ryan, J. E. (2010). *Five miles away, a world apart: One city, two schools, and the story of educational opportunity in modern America.* New York, NY: Oxford University Press.

Saiger, A. (2006). The last wave: The rise of the contingent school district. *North Carolina Law Review, 84,* 857–926.

Saiger, A. (2010). The school district boundary problem. *Urban Lawyer, 42,* 495–550.

Saltman, K. (2010). *Urban school decentralization and the growth of 'Portfolio Districts.'* East Lansing, MI: Great Lakes Center for Education Research and Policy.

Sartain, L., McGhee, R., Jr. Cassidy, L., Abasi, M. I., Young, V. M., Sporte, S. E., & Shields, P. M. (2009). *High school reform in Chicago public schools: Autonomous management and performance schools.* Menlo Park, CA: SRI International.

Tennessee Code Annot. §49-16-204 (2013).

U.S. Government Accountability Office (GAO). (2012). *Charter schools: Additional federal attention needed to help protect access for students with disabilities.* Washington, DC: Author.

Wong, K. K., & Shen, F. X. (2013). *Mayoral governance and student achievement: How mayor-led districts are improving school and student performance.* Washington, DC: Center for American Progress.

CHAPTER 2

CAN FAITH-BASED CHARTER SCHOOLS SURVIVE CONSTITUTIONAL CHALLENGES?[1]

Charles J. Russo and Gerald M. Cattaro

INTRODUCTION

In light of Establishment Clause concerns, it is unlikely that faith-based, or religiously affiliated charter schools, can survive constitutional challenges. Significant state restrictions forbid aid to religious institutions insofar as state laws typically prevent religious entities from operating charter schools. As such, it is improbable that religious charter schools can withstand judicial scrutiny in federal courts, and are likely to be struck down in state courts.

The charter school movement, which began in 1991 in Minnesota, has spread to forty-two jurisdictions plus Puerto Rico and the District of Columbia (Center for Education Reform, n.d.). Charter schools, public schools of choice, typically function as independent districts consisting of single schools operated by private groups. These groups may include parents

Law and Education Inequality, pages 19–31

religiously affiliated nonpublic schools. Without actually using the words "Child Benefit" Test, the Supreme Court reasoned that it was permissible to extend a general benefit such as transportation to all children (and their parents) without regard to their religious beliefs. In language presaging future developments, in which it would take a hard line against most forms of aid, Justice Black's majority opinion introduced the Jeffersonian metaphor, declaring that "The First Amendment has erected a wall between church and state. That wall must be kept high and impregnable. We could not approve the slightest breach" (Everson v. Board of Education, 1947, p. 18).

In *Board of Education of Central School District No. 1 v. Allen* (1968), the Supreme Court upheld the constitutionality of a law from New York requiring local boards to loan textbooks for instruction in secular subjects to children in grades 7 to 12 who attended nonpublic schools. The statute did not specify that the books had to be the same as those used in the public schools but did require local public school board officials to approve their use before adoption. The Court held that the law was constitutional because its purpose was neither to aid religion nor nonpublic schools and that its primary effect was to improve the quality of education for all children.

The Supreme Court sustained the constitutionality of similar textbook provisions from Pennsylvania in *Meek v. Pittenger* (1975) and Ohio in *Wolman v. Walter* (1977) but struck down loans of instructional materials such as library books, computers, television sets, tape recorders, and maps to nonpublic schools. Until the Supreme Court allowed the delivery of services to individual students as in *Zobrest v. Catalina Foothills School District* (1993), *Allen* was the outer limit of the Child Benefit Test.

The Static Years

Following their success in *Everson* and *Allen,* proponents of the Child Benefit Test supported laws in Pennsylvania and Rhode Island, respectively, dealing with a different form of aid. Both statutes provided assistance to religiously affiliated nonpublic schools in the form of salary supplements for teachers in nonpublic schools, an issue that would certainly emerge in disputes involving religious charter schools. In a case that has come to represent the standard test in Establishment Clause cases, whether aid or prayer and religious activities in schools, *Lemon v. Kurtzman* (1971), the Court invalidated both laws, ushering in an era of strict adherence to the Jeffersonian wall of separation of church and state.

In creating the tripartite measure known as the *Lemon* test, the Supreme Court combined tests from two of its earlier cases. The first two parts came from the 1963 companion cases of *Abington v. Schempp and Murray v.*

Curlett, wherein the Justices struck down prayer and Bible reading in public schools. The third element, prohibiting excessive entanglement, came from from *Walz v. Tax Commission of New York City* (1970), which upheld New York State's practice of providing state property tax exemptions for church property used in worship services. Under this test,

> Every analysis in this area must begin with consideration of the cumulative criteria developed by the Court over many years. Three such tests may be gleaned from our cases. First, the statute must have a secular legislative purpose; second, its principal or primary effect must be one that neither advances nor inhibits religion; finally, the statute must not foster "an excessive government entanglement with religion." (pp. 612–613)

As to entanglement, the Court specified that "we must examine the character and purposes of the institutions that are benefitted, the nature of the aid that the State provides, and the resulting relationship between the government and religious authority" (p. 615).

As illustrated by the final case during the second phase in the history of the Child Benefit test, *Aguilar v. Felton* (1985), most statutes passed *Lemon's* first two prongs, but ran afoul of the excessive entanglement test, highlighting the fact that programs must pass all three of the independent prongs. In *Aguilar,* a judgment reminiscent of *Meek* and *Wolman,* the Court struck down on-site delivery of Title I services designed to provide remedial instruction for poor children who attended religious schools in New York City (NYC) based solely on the fear of entanglement absent allegations of inappropriate conduct. The two decades following *Lemon* were static from the perspective of proponents of the Child Benefit Test as the Supreme Court refused to move beyond the limits it created in *Everson* and *Allen.*

The Reinvigoration of the Child Benefit Test

Witters v. Washington Department of Services for the Blind (1986), a case from higher education, was a harbinger of change in the Supreme Court's Establishment Clause jurisprudence. In *Witters,* the Court upheld the constitutionality of a program of general vocational assistance to a blind man who was studying to become a clergyman at a religious college.

In *Zobrest v. Catalina Foothills School District* (1993), the Justices began the reinvigoration of the Child Benefit Test for K–12 schools, allowing it to enter a phase that extends through the present. In *Zobrest,* the Court permitted the on-site delivery of a sign-language interpreter under the Individuals with Disabilities Education Act (IDEA, 2014) for a deaf student in Arizona who sought to attend a Catholic high school. The Court decided that insofar as the interpreter provided neutral aid to the student without offering financial benefits to his parents or school and there was no governmental participation in the instruction because the interpreter was only a conduit to effectuate the child's communications, he was entitled to the aid.

A year after *Zobrest*, though, the Supreme Court affirmed the unconstitutionality of a law from New York which created a school district that was contiguous with the boundaries of the village inhabited by members of a religious community. The law was designed to accommodate the needs of parents of children with disabilities so that their young would not have to be transported outside of their community to receive educational services under the IDEA. In *Board of Education of Kiryas Joel Village School District v. Grumet* (1994), the Court struck the law down on the ground that the board could have offered appropriate special education programs at one of its public schools or at a neutral site near one of the village's religious schools due to risk of too close of an association between religion and the state.

Days after the Supreme Court struck down the statute in *Kiryas Joel*, the New York State legislature amended the law in an attempt to eliminate the Establishment Clause problem. Still, the Court of Appeals of New York (Grumet v. Cuomo, 1997) struck down the statute for violating the Establishment Clause insofar as it had the effect of advancing one religion.

The most significant post-*Lemon* change in the Supreme Court's Establishment Clause analysis occurred in 1997 in *Agostini*. The Court held that the on-site delivery of Title I programs to students in faith-based schools in NYC did not violate the test it used to consider whether state aid advanced religion where there was no governmental indoctrination, there were no distinctions between recipients based on religion, and there was no excessive entanglement between religion and government.

The Supreme Court explained that a federal program designed to provide supplemental, remedial instruction and counseling services to disadvantaged children on a neutral basis is not unconstitutional when the assistance is provided on-site in religiously affiliated nonpublic schools pursuant to a program containing safeguards such as those that the NYC Board of Education had created. The most significant jurisprudential development in *Agostini* was that the Court modified the *Lemon* test by reviewing only its first two parts, purpose and effect, while recasting entanglement as one element in evaluating the statute's effect.

Three years later, in *Mitchell v. Helms* (2000), a case from Louisiana, the Supreme Court expanded the limits of aid to religiously affiliated nonpublic schools. A plurality agreed on the rationale, expressly repudiating those parts of *Meek* and *Wolman* to the contrary, upholding the constitutionality of a federal statute permitting loans of instructional materials, including library books, computers, television sets, tape recorders, and maps, to nonpublic schools. Relying largely on the hybrid *Agostini* test, the Court pointed out that insofar as the statute's purpose was not in dispute, it only had to consider the law's effect. The Court found that the statute did not foster impermissible indoctrination because aid was allocated pursuant to neutral secular criteria that neither favored nor disfavored religion and was available to all schools based on secular, nondiscriminatory grounds.

The final Supreme Court case with direct relevance to religious charter schools is *Zelman v. Simmons-Harris* (2002). In *Zelman*, the Court upheld a voucher program from Ohio that was part of a larger plan for helping poor students in Cleveland's failing public schools that had been taken over by the state as part of a desegregation remedy. Again relying on *Agostini*, the Court addressed "whether the government acted with the purpose of advancing or inhibiting religions [and] whether the aid has the 'effect' of advancing or inhibiting religion" (p. 649).

Recognizing that the voucher program in *Zelman* had a valid secular purpose in providing aid for poor children, the Supreme Court examined whether it had the impermissible effect of advancing religion. The Justices upheld the voucher program as constitutional. As part of the state's far-reaching attempt to provide greater educational opportunities for students in a failing school system, the voucher program allocated aid pursuant to neutral secular criteria that neither favored nor disfavored religion, was available to both religious and secular recipients on a nondiscriminatory grounds, and offered assistance directly to a broad class of citizens who directed the aid to religious schools based entirely on their own genuine and independent private choices. The Court was satisfied that the law included safeguards so that tuition checks were sent to parents who signed them over to schools such that there was no direct exchange of funds between religious schools and the state.

The Justices were unconcerned over that fact that most parents sent their children to religiously affiliated nonpublic schools because surrounding public school boards refused to participate in the program. As such, the Supreme Court held that insofar as parents sent their children to the religiously affiliated nonpublic schools not as a matter of law but since they were unwelcomed in the public schools, the program was constitutional. The Court concluded that insofar as it was following an unbroken line of its own precedent supporting private choice providing benefits directly to needy private individuals, the voucher program was constitutional. Not surprisingly, post-*Zelman* suits challenging vouchers focused on state constitutional grounds, with mixed results, because they are typically more stringent than under their federal counterpart.

Legal Issues

As the number of religiously affiliated nonpublic schools declines, supporters of faith-based charter schools will undoubtedly step up their efforts to circumvent existing judicial precedent, statutes, and/or constitutional provisions restricting their ability to operate such schools. Yet, regardless of whether challengers apply the *Lemon* test or its hybrid *Agostini* version, precedent demonstrates the unlikelihood of surmounting challenges confronting supporters of faith-based charter schools under Establishment Clause scrutiny.

The probability that laws creating religious charter schools will be struck down is real because it is difficult to maintain that they can satisfy the requirements of having secular legislative purposes, avoiding the advancement of religion, and/or sidestepping concerns with excessive entanglement of religion and government. Further, to the extent that faith-based charter schools would be seeking public funds, their religious practices would come under intense scrutiny insofar as the application of "control follows the dollar" would require closer oversight by governmental bodies, thereby exacerbating the constitutional difficulties, especially with regard to entanglement.

As individuals and/or groups seek to operate religious charter schools, they are likely to face myriad legal challenges on such key issues as governance, parental choice, and the place of prayer and religious activity in schools and curricula. As to governance, to the extent that Catholic schools, for instance, are typically part of larger parish legal corporations, it is unclear how transfers of titles would be viewed legally, especially if religious leaders were involved in establishing governing boards. That is, insofar as governance corresponds to the set of policies and customs by which organizations are controlled, thus ensuring representation by stakeholders, it is unclear what role the government would have in arrangements of this nature.

At the same time, when applied to faith-based charter schools, governance suggests that some other body is in control such as an independent governing board that may not share the beliefs of parents who wish to send their children to these schools. Consequently, while faith-based charter schools may offer opportunities for streamlined models of educational delivery and site-based control similar to what occurs in religiously affiliated nonpublic schools, they must rely on outside bodies, or boards, of control. Even though religious institutions, acting as sponsors, may provide buildings and agencies for charter schools, they are unlikely to be exempt from the control issues related to not-for-profit boards, state statutes, and federal guidelines.

Faith-based charter schools are also likely to face questions with the potential to impact significantly on their missions and identities, especially if they formerly operated as religiously affiliated nonpublic schools. For example, how many parents of students in faith-based charter schools will not be parishioners or even members of their faith communities? If faculty members are to serve as role models, who will define what it means to do so, particularly in the context of Title VII and exceptions that allow religious employers to hire members of their own faiths? Whose health curriculum, relating to such matters as birth control and abortion, will have to be taught? Will administrators and teachers be viewed as ministers of the faith or agents of the State?

Additional questions are likely to emerge pursuant to the notion that parents choose to send their children to religious charter schools based on their own independent private choices.

The notion of parental choice that the Supreme Court accepted in *Zelman* notwithstanding, challengers will raise questions over the extent to which such independent decision-making measures up with the requisite safeguards that need to be in place to avoid entanglement between religion and government, regardless of whether one applies the original *Lemon* or its modification in *Agostini.* Further, as reflected in *Kiryas Joel,* even when public officials try to accommodate sincerely held parental religious beliefs for the benefit of their children, Establishment Clause issues can come to the fore that would invalidate what may appear to be reasonable requests designed for the best educational interest of students.

Other significant challenges to religious charter schools will surface in connection with interrelated concerns dealing with prayer and religious activity, religious artifacts/iconography in schools, and curricular content/control. Serious concerns arise here under the purpose, effect, and entanglement prongs of *Lemon-Agostini,* especially in light of potential allegations that educators have advanced religion, a claim that has already surfaced in connection with the instructional program at a Muslim charter school in Minnesota, where a federal trial court found that its proposed curriculum violated the Establishment Clause (*American Civil Liberties Union of Minnesota v. Tarek Ibn Ziyad Academy,* 2011).

Complying with case law will undoubtedly require educational leaders to prevent prayer and religious activity from taking place in faith-based charter schools, the posting of religious artifacts/iconography in schools, and instruction about religion from curricula, changes that would fundamentally modify their nature and missions. In this light, it is mystifying why Catholic religious leaders have embarked on such an approach. While it may be admirable that these leaders tried to ensure the survival of the diversity that their schools provide in the educational marketplace of ideas, at what cost are they doing so? Are they essentially creating faith-based charter schools that probably cannot teach about religion? In other words, to the extent that religiously affiliated nonpublic schools, especially at the elementary school level, are dedicated to the inculcation of the beliefs of their faiths, it remains to be seen how these institutions can survive judicial challenges if they teach about religion.

Turning to religion in curricula, it is unclear why educational leaders in religious institutions would seek to move to a faith-based charter school model insofar as they will have lost substantial, if not total, control over school operations. A related question is whether courts would treat transfers in ownership in title over buildings as sham transactions essentially designed to accomplish educational-curricular goals that they had previously been prohibited from pursuing. Further, even if one places the issue of ownership and control aside—insofar as charter schools are public schools, albeit ones that are free from many state requirements, and it is well settled that they can teach about religion but cannot teach religion per se—disputes are likely to emerge over how pervasive religion is in school curricula.

CONCLUSION

The well-intentioned efforts of their supporters notwithstanding, the combination of constitutional and statutory prohibitions, in conjunction with long-standing judicial precedent, make it clear that organizers of faith-based charter schools are unlikely to succeed. Clearly, such an outcome is likely to be disappointing to parents who wish to have their children educated in faith-based environments. Yet such a result may well be better for the schools themselves and families wishing to have their children educated in religiously affiliated schools because by keeping the state at arm's length, particularly with regard to curricular content, educators can be free to teach students in environments free from governmental intervention.

NOTE

1. This chapter is adapted from a much lengthier article that appeared as Russo & Cattaro, 2009.

REFERENCES

Abington v. Schempp and Murray v. Curlett, 374 U.S. 203 (1963).
Agostini v. Felton, 521 U.S. 203 (1997).
Aguilar v. Felton, 473 U.S. 402 (1985).
American Civil Liberties Union of Minnesota v. Tarek Ibn Ziyad Academy, 788 F. Supp.2d 950 (D. Minn. 2011).
Board of Education of Central School District No. 1 v. Allen, 392 U.S. 236 (1968).

Board of Education of Kiryas Joel Village School District v. Grumet, 512 U.S. 687 (1994).

Cantwell v. Connecticut, 310 U.S. 296 (1940).

Center for Education Reform. (n.d.). *Choice and charter schools.* Bethesda, MD: Author. Retrieved on January 26, 2015, from https://www.edreform.com/issues/choice-charter-schools/laws-legislation/

Everson v. Board of Education, 330 U.S. 1 (1947), *reh'g denied,* 330 U.S. 855 (1947).

Grumet v. Cuomo, 659 N.Y.S.2d 173, 681 N.E.2d 340 (1997); Grumet v. Pataki, 697 N.Y.S.2d846 (1999), *cert. denied,* 528 U.S. 946, 120 S. Ct. 363, 145 L.Ed.2d 284 (1999).

Individuals with Disabilities Act, 20 U.S.C.A. §§ 1400 *et seq.* (2014).

Lemon v. Kurtzman, 403 U.S. 602 (1971).

Meek v. Pittenger, 421 U.S. 349 (1975).

Mitchell v. Helms, 530 U.S. 793 (2000), *reh'g denied,* 530 U.S. 1296 (2000), on remand sub nom. Helms v. Picard, 229 F.3d 467 (5th Cir. 2000).

Ohio Revised Code, Ohio Rev. Code § 3314.03(11)(c) (2014).

Pierce v. Society of Sisters of the Holy Names of Jesus and Mary, 268 U.S. 510 (1925).

Russo, C. J., & Cattaro, G. M. (2009). Faith-based charter schools: An idea whose time is unlikely to come. *Religion & Education, 36*(1), 72–93.

Walz v. Tax Commission of New York City, 397 U.S. 664 (1970).

Witters v. Washington Department of Services for the Blind, 474 U.S. 481 (1986).

Wolman v. Walter, 433 U.S. 229 (1977).

Zelman v. Simmons-Harris, 536 U.S. 639 (2002).

Zobrest v. Catalina Foothills School District, 509 U.S. 1 (1993).

CHAPTER 3

BEYOND LEGAL REMEDIES

Toward Funding Equity and Improved Educational Opportunities for English Language Learners

Carrie Sampson and Sonya Douglass Horsford

An essential component of the "American Dream," the U.S. public education system carries the considerable responsibility of preparing a richly diverse student population for academic proficiency, economic mobility, and life success. Given the dynamic and evolving nature of the nation's racial, ethnic, and cultural diversity, it should not be surprising that many American schoolchildren speak a language other than English at home. Nearly 1 in every 10 public school students (roughly 4.5 million of 50 million total students) was classified as an English Language learner[1] (ELL) during the 2010–2011 school year (DOE, 2013a). ELL students have the potential to be an incredible asset for the United States, yet some states and school districts have treated these students as a burden. In certain cases, school districts have discriminated against them. Although the Civil Rights Act of 1964 legally protects ELL students, it was not until the institution of the Equal Education Opportunities Act (EEOA) of 1974 that the federal

Law and Education Inequality, pages 35–48

government required states and school districts to ensure ELL students had access to an equal education (DOJ, n.d.).

LEGAL BATTLES AND REMEDIES FOR ENGLISH LANGUAGE LEARNERS

Prior to this mandate, the federal government provided supplemental funding for school districts to create "new and imaginative" (DOJ, n.d., sec. 702) programs for ELL students through the Bilingual Education Act (BEA) of 1968 (now known as Title III of the Elementary and Secondary Education Act). However, after the Supreme Court determined that nearly 1,800 Chinese ELL students in San Francisco were wrongly denied the necessary resources to attain the same education as their non-ELL peers in *Lau v. Nichols* (1974), schools receiving federal dollars under BEA were expected to adopt guidelines referred to the *Lau Remedies*, which included classification, instruction, and teacher preparation related to ELL education and supported bilingual measures of teaching and learning. This case, along with others, created a legal basis for educational equity and financial adequacy pertaining to ELL students, meaning that schools must invest adequate and perhaps additional resources to ELL education so that ELL students would lawfully receive equal educational opportunities regardless of race, color, or national origin (de Jong, 2013; Li, 2007).

In 1981, the Reagan Administration suspended the *Lau Remedies* largely due to the resistance toward bilingual education (Duignan, 1996; Ochoa, 1995) and since then, ELL programs have been held to the "Castañeda Test" by courts and agencies. This test was the result of the *Castañeda v. Pickard* (1981) decision by the Fifth Circuit Court of Appeals in favor of Mexican American students and their families who sued a Texas school district for racial segregation and not providing bilingual services, therefore violating the EEOA. Under this test's standards, ELL programs must (a) be developed using theory, (b) have sufficient support, and (c) include an assessment that demonstrates the program's effectiveness. Critics recognize that the ambiguity inherent in the Castañeda standards not only leads to great variations in ELL programs and services, it can ultimately deprive ELL students of a quality education (Del Valle, 2003; Johansen, 2009; López & McEneaney, 2012). For instance, most educational programs can be theoretically supported with minimal funding and resources, yet these might not be the most effective programs to institute and can even produce negative outcomes. Furthermore, deficiencies in ELL programs might take years to identify through assessments, therefore any potential shortcomings could have a significant impact on the education of ELL students long before ever being addressed.

After over 20 years of litigation, *Horne v. Flores* (2009) is one of the most recent legal battles to shape ELL education and exemplifies the significance of ELL funding. This case was filed in 1992 by parents of ELL students who claimed that Arizona had not provided their children with the resources (i.e., qualified teachers, instruction, and adequate funding) to reach proficiency in the schools' academic content (Flores v. Arizona, 2000; Rios-Aguilar & Gándara, 2012). The District Court sided with the plaintiffs and ordered the Arizona Legislature to conduct a costing-out study to determine what would be a sufficient funding level for ELL education (Arizona State Senate, 2008; Flores v. Arizona, 2000). Prior to this, Arizona allocated $150 per ELL pupil, which the Court determined was "arbitrary and capricious" when compared to the resources necessary for ELL students to achieve academic proficiency (Flores v. Arizona, 2005). Although the costing-out study suggested funding ranging from $0 to $4,600 per ELL pupil, the Arizona Legislature increased the amount to $340 in 2001 and then conducted another costing-out study (Arizona State Senate, 2008; Iddings, Combs, & Moll, 2012).

In early 2005, the second costing-out study determined that a range of $670 to $2,571 per ELL pupil was adequate funding (Arizona State Senate, 2008; Iddings et al., 2012). To implement these recommendations, the Legislature proposed an increase in funding, which was vetoed by Arizona's Governor (Arizona State Senate, 2008; Iddings et al., 2012). By the end of 2005, the District Court responded by imposing more than $20 million in fines on the state following a 5-year noncompliance of the court order (Horne v. Flores, 2009). Eventually, on March 2, 2006, Arizona increased the ELL funding to $432 per pupil and created an ELL task force to develop a structured English immersion model instituted in 2007 (Arizona State Senate, 2008). On April 27, 2006, the District Court determined that the funding for this program was insufficient. After a series of appeals, the District Court ultimately sided with the defendants and made a final decision to vacate its earlier judgment on March 29, 2013 (ACLPI, 2013). The case came to a close following 21 years of litigation and a significant cost to ELL students and the state of Arizona. Legal battles such as these demonstrate the fact that it can take years to make sufficient changes, likely having detrimental effects on ELL education in the meantime.

THE GROWING SIGNIFICANCE OF EDUCATIONAL OPPORTUNITY AND EQUITY FOR ELL STUDENTS

While states such as California, Texas, Florida, and New York benefit from the experience of serving large numbers of ELL students, a growing number of states are only more recently considering what it means to serve this

TABLE 3.1 Comparison of ELL Enrollment, Growth, and Funding in 10 Fastest-Growing ELL States From 2000 to 2010

State	ELL Enrollment 2000–2001	ELL Enrollment 2010–2011	% Change in ELLs from 2000–2001 to 2010–2011	Total State ELL-Specified Funding in 2010–2011 (unless otherwise noted)	Dollars Spent Per ELL Student Beyond Regular Per-Pupil Funding 2010–2011	State Funding Mechanism/Allocation
U.S. Total	**3,707,689**	**4,371,553**	**18%**			**N/A**
South Carolina	5,121	36,379	610%	—	—	No state funding.
Kentucky	4,030	16,351	306%	$5,900,000	$375	The state total and per-ELL-pupil dollar amounts are based on the 2011–2012 school year ELL count of 15,720 students used to allocate a specific state grant for ELL services.
Nevada	23,488	83,352	255%	—	—	No state funding.
Delaware	2,081	6,858	230%	$1,336,143	$195	Funding is based on the number of qualifying students (including ELLs), which are calculated into units used for instructional salaries. Units can also be cashed out for other services. These dollar figures are an overestimate, because students cannot be counted more than once for unit-based funding.
Arkansas	11,847	31,537	166%	$9,240,341	$293	Funding is distributed to school districts per identified ELL student. In FY2012 the state changed funding to $305 according to Arkansas General Assembly Act 1039 of 2011; was $293 from 2007–2008 until FY 2012.

(continued)

TABLE 3.1 Comparison of ELL Enrollment, Growth, and Funding in 10 Fastest-Growing ELL States From 2000 to 2010 (continued)

State	ELL Enrollment 2000–2001	ELL Enrollment 2010–2011	% Change in ELLs from 2000–2001 to 2010–2011	Total State ELL-Specified Funding in 2010–2011 (unless otherwise noted)	Dollars Spent Per ELL Student Beyond Regular Per-Pupil Funding 2010–2011	State Funding Mechanism/Allocation
Kansas	14,878	39,323	164%	$18,435,000	$469	Funding is based on the total number of ELL contact hours per district, determined by either a full-day, pull-out program or paraprofessional/in-class support models, and then calculated within a specified formula.
Mississippi	2,176	5,620	158%	—	—	No state funding.
Alabama	7,226	17,559	143%	$2,288,011	$130	State allocations are provided according to the ELL student count in the prior year.
Virginia	36,802	88,033	139%	$38,885,716	$442	Funding is based on a formula of 17 teachers per 1,000 ELL students multiplied by 1 minus a composite index. Supports instructional positions for ELL students to be shared with local schools.
North Carolina	44,087	103,249	134%	$76,536,814	$741	Funding through categorical programs used to hire personnel, provide services, or purchase supplies. Funding varies based on the number of ELLs and the concentration of ELLs in local education agencies (LEAs).

Note: Dollar figures are rounded to the nearest dollar. Ohio was not included due to inconsistent figures. California, North Dakota, and Tennessee did not report ELL numbers to NCES for one or both years.

Sources: Alabama Legislative Fiscal Office, 2012; Arkansas Department of Education, 2013; DOE, 2013a, n.d.; DOE, NCES 2012; Kansas State Department of Education, 2008; Kentucky Department of Education, 2013; North Carolina Department of Public Instruction, 2011; State of Delaware, 2012; Verstegen, 2011; Virginia Department of Education, 2012.

ELL states (respectively): South Carolina, Kentucky, Nevada, Delaware, Arkansas, Kansas, Mississippi, Alabama, Virginia, and North Carolina.

Although these 10 states vary widely in their ELL enrollment and ELL programs, they have experienced extreme growth in their ELL populations in just one decade. Collectively, they reflect the great variation in how states approach ELL education.

Dollars spent per ELL student beyond a state's regular per-pupil funding expenditure level varied greatly based on both funding mechanism and level. In order to provide some comparison of how states funded educational opportunities for their ELL students, we collected per-ELL-pupil funding figures as reported directly by states, as well as calculated figures for non-reporting states by identifying that state's total budget for ELL-related services and resources and dividing that figure by the state's ELL enrollment count for the corresponding year as reported by the NCES. Some states base their budgets on specialized formulas, which we used to arrive at an estimated average per-ELL-pupil figure. For instance, Delaware uses "units for academic excellence" to determine additional funding for at-risk populations (Del. Code educ, 2015). Each unit is based on 250 full-time K–12 students who qualify for additional services and programs, such as ELL students. Units can be used toward personnel, and up to 30% of the units can be cashed out for $35,000 per unit to pay for services. We estimated Delaware's per-ELL spending based on the 2010–2011 ELL count of 6,858 students, equaling approximately 27.5 units, reported salary expenditures in FY 2010 that averaged $54,410 per salary, and assumed 30% of the units were cashed out for a total $288,750 (State of Delaware, 2012). Using these calculations, we estimated that Delaware spent approximately $1,336,142 on ELL education, which amounts to about $195 per ELL pupil. This figure is most likely overestimated based on the fact that some ELL students may also qualify for other services under the "units of academic excellence," such as those for gifted and talented or at-risk students, but can only be counted once according to the state law.

Although these figures reflect publicly available budgets and data for ELL students, it is difficult to compare state ELL funding levels due to the variations in how states collect and report ELL data (with figures that are also different from what are reported in national databases), in addition to the various approaches used to fund ELL education. These approaches include everything from additional per-pupil dollars and weighted formulas to block grants or "lump sums," all of which vary in amount from state to state (Horsford et al., 2013). This exercise, in coming up with comparable ELL spending figures, reiterates the need for more transparency and equity in funding ELL education.

Of the states highlighted in Table 3.1, South Carolina reflects the largest share of ELL population growth between the 2000–2001 and 2010–2011 school years at 610%. Ironically, however, like Mississippi and Nevada, South Carolina does not provide any state dollars to fund ELL education. In contrast, North Carolina and Virginia, which have each seen their ELL populations more than triple over the last decade, provide $741 and $401, respectively, per ELL student. And as noted in Table 3.1, some states do not fund ELL education at all, relying mainly on federal funding, which averaged $180 per ELL pupil in 2010–2011 (DOE, n.d.). Despite being a high-ELL-growth state and having the highest density of ELL students of any state in the country, Nevada counts itself among those states that do not fund ELL education, further illustrating the severe inability of the state to meet the evident needs of nearly one third of its overall student population.

FUNDING EDUCATIONAL OPPORTUNITY AND EQUITY

Sadly, the fact that states have focused for more than 30 years on standards and accountability, absent the resources and investments needed to achieve those standards and to sustain success, reflects a major flaw in state-level education policy. The result is a system adept at labeling failure but incapable of doing anything about it. As noted in our comparison of high-ELL-growth states, funding levels, mechanisms, and allocations vary widely, making it difficult to determine how funding and student achievement are monitored and who gets what and whether or not funding translates into improved student achievement. Perhaps most important is the fact that a much-needed focus on equity in education policy, and particularly on state-funding equity (Baker, Sciarra, & Farrie, 2012; DOE, 2013b), reflects the pendulum swinging back to what the Elementary and Secondary Education Act originally intended—the provision of increased federal resources for disadvantaged schools and students and an emphasis on access to equal education.

In Gándara and Rumberger's (2007) costing-out study of linguistic minorities in California, the researchers utilized a definition of adequacy that they described as *reclassification and maintenance of academic proficiency*, which moves students from ELL to Fluent English Proficiency status while providing resources until all students receiving support become proficient in other academic content. The schools in their pilot study were included based on high levels of ELL academic achievement, location, and curriculum. The study identified five areas that require investment for ELL success:

- A high-quality preschool program;
- A comprehensive instructional program that addresses both English language development and the core curriculum;
- Sufficient and appropriate student and family support;

Arizona Center for Law in the Public Interest (ACLPI). (2013). *Flores v. Huppenthal et.al.* Phoenix, AZ: Author. Retrieved from http://aclpi.org/case/flores-v-huppenthal-et-al

Arizona Department of Education. (2001). *English acquisition program cost study: Phases I through IV.* Phoenix, AZ: Author.

Arizona State Senate. (2008, August 27). *Issue paper: Flores v. Arizona.* Retrieved from http://www.azleg.gov/briefs/Senate/FLORES%20V.%20ARIZONA.pdf

Arkansas Department of Education. (2013). *How are school districts in Arkansas funded?* Retrieved from http://www.arkansased.org/faqs/1/how-are-school-districts-in-arkansas-funded

Baker, B., Sciarra, D., & Farrie, D. (2012). *Is school funding fair? A national report card.* Newark, NJ: Education Law Center. Retrieved from http://files.eric.ed.gov/fulltext/ ED533413.pdf

Castañeda v. Pickard, 648 F. 2d 989 (5th Cir. 1981).

de Jong, E. J. (2013). Policy discourses and U.S. language in education policies. *Peabody Journal of Education, 88*(1), 98–111.

Del. Code educ. 17, *§ 1716* (2015).

Del Valle, S. (2003). *Language rights and the law in the United States.* Tonawanda, NY: Multilingual Matters.

Doughman, A. (2013, May 1). Education advocates threaten lawsuit over funding public schools. *Las Vegas Sun.* Retrieved from http://www.lasvegassun.com/news/2013/may/01/education-advocates-threaten-lawsuit-over-public-s/

Duignan, P. J. (1998, September 1). Bilingual education: A critique. *Hoover Institution, Stanford University.* Retrieved from http://www.hoover.org/publications/monographs/27198

Epstein, N. (1992). Affirmative ethnicity. In J. Crawford (Ed.), *Language loyalties: A source book on the official English controversy* (pp. 334–341). Chicago, IL: University of Chicago Press.

Flores v. Arizona, 172 F. Supp. 2d 1225 (D. Ariz. 2000).

Flores v. Arizona, 405 F. Supp. 2d 1112 (D. Ariz. 2005).

Gándara, P., & Hopkins, M. (Eds.). (2010). *Forbidden language: English learners and restrictive language.* New York, NY: Teachers College Press.

Gándara, P., & Rumberger, R. (2006). *Resource needs for California English learners.* Sacramento, CA: Linguistic Minority Research Institute.

Gándara, P., & Rumberger, R. (2007). *Resource needs for California English learners: Getting down to facts project summary.* Stanford, CA: Institute for Research on Education Policy and Practice.

Gándara, P., & Rumberger, R. (2008). Defining an adequate education for English learners. *Education Finance and Policy, 3,* 130–148.

Hanushek, E. (1997). Assessing the effects of school resources on student performance: An update. *Educational Evaluation and Policy Analysis, 19*(2), 141–164.

Horne v. Flores, 129 S. Ct. 2579–Supreme Court 2009

Horsford, S. D., Mokhtar, C., & Sampson, C. (2013). Nevada's English language learners: A review of enrollment, outcomes, and opportunities. *UNLV/The Lincy Institute.* Retrieved from www.unlv.edu/sites/default/files/24/Lincy-EducationSector-ELL-FullReport.pdf

Iddings, A. C. D., Combs, M. C., & Moll, L. (2012). In the arid zone: Drying out educational resources for English language learners through policy and practice. *Urban Education, 47*(2), 495–514.

Jimenez-Castellanos, O., & Topper, A. M. (2012). The cost of providing an adequate education to English language learners: A review of the literature. *Review of Educational Research, 82*(2), 179–232.

Johansen, I. M. (2009). Legal requirements on access to elementary and secondary public education for children of immigrants. *Popular Government, 74*(3), 35–39.

Kansas State Department of Education (2009). *Kansas English speakers of other languages (ESOL) bilingual education funding.* Retrieved from http://www.ksde.org/Portals/0/Early%20Childhood/State%20PreKindergarten/CriteriaESOL-BilingualKSFunding.pdf

Kentucky Department of Education. (2013, January 9). *Kentucky education facts.* Retrieved from http://education.ky.gov/comm/edfacts/Pages/default.aspx

Lau v. Nichols, 414 US 563–Supreme Court 1974

Li, B. (2007). From bilingual education to OELALEAALEPS: How the No Child Left Behind Act has undermined English language learners' access to a meaningful education. *Georgetown Journal on Poverty Law & Policy, 14*(3), 539–572.

López, F., & McEneaney, E. (2012). State implementation of language acquisition policies and reading achievement among Hispanic students. *Educational Policy, 26*(4), 418–464.

Migration Policy Institute (2010). http://www.migrationpolicy.org/sites/default/files/publications/FactSheet%20ELL2%20-%20FINAL.pdf

Multicultural Education Training and Advocacy, Inc. (2008). *Getting it right: Ensuring a quality education for English language learners in New York.* Prepared by the New York Immigration Coalition. Retrieved from http://www.edweek.org/media/nyic_ellbrief_final.pdf

National Access Network. (2010, June). *Litigations challenging constitutionality of K–12 funding in the 50 states.* New York, NY: Teachers College, Columbia University. Retrieved from www.schoolfunding.info/litigation/New_Charts/06_2010_lit_chall_constitutionality.pdf

National Conference of State Legislatures. (2005, February). *Arizona English language learner cost study.* Prepared for the Arizona Legislative Council. Retrieved from http://www.schoolfunding.info/states/az/AZ-NCSLenglanglearn2005.pdf

North Carolina Department of Public Instruction. (2011). Information analysis, division of school business: Highlights of the North Carolina public school budget. Retrieved from www.dpi.state.nc.us

Ochoa, A. M. (1995). Language policy and social implications for addressing the bicultural immigrant experience in the United States. In A. Darder (Ed.), *Culture and difference: Critical perspectives on the bicultural experience in the United States* (pp. 227–254). Westport, CT: Green.

Rios-Aguilar, C., & Gándara, P. (2012). *Horne v. Flores* and the future of language policy. *Teachers College Record, 114*(9), 1–13.

State of Delaware. (2012). *Budget archive: FY2011.* Dover, DE: Author. Retrieved from http://budget.delaware.gov/fy2011/budget2011.shtml

U.S. Department of Education (DOE). (2013a). *ED facts/Consolidated state performance reports, 2010–11.* Retrieved from http://www2.ed.gov/admins/lead/account/consolidated/index.html

U.S. Department of Education (DOE). (2013b). *For each and every child: A strategy for education equity and excellence.* Retrieved from http://www2.ed.gov/about/bdscomm/list/eec/equity-excellence-commission-report.pdf

U.S. Department of Education (DOE). (n.d.). *ED data express: Data about elementary & secondary schools in the U.S. state tables.* Retrieved from http://eddataexpress.ed.gov/state-tables-main.cfm

U.S. Department of Education, National Center for Education Statistics (DOE, NCES). (2012). *The condition of education 2012.* Retrieved from http://nces.ed.gov/pubs2012/2012045.pdf

U.S. Department of Education (DOE), Office of Civil Rights (OCR). (2013). *The total number of complaints filed to the Office of Civil Rights, U.S. Department of Education regarding English language learners (or Limited English Proficient students) by state and the U.S.* A Freedom of Information Act Request. Control # 13-024243.

U.S. Department of Education, Office of Planning, Evaluation and Policy Development, Policy and Program Studies Service. (2012) *National evaluation of Title III implementation—Report on state and local implementation.* Retrieved from http://www2.ed.gov/about/offices/list/opepd/ppss/reports.html#titleiii

U.S. Department of Justice (DOJ). (n.d.). *Types of educational opportunities discrimination.* Retrieved from http://www.justice.gov/crt/about/edu/types.php

Verstegen, D. A. (2011). *A quick glance at school finance: A 50 state survey of school finance policies.* Retrieved from http://schoolfinancesdav.wordpress.com

Virginia Department of Education. (2012). *School finance: Overview of standards of quality funding process.* Richmond, VA: Author. Retrieved from http://www.doe.virginia.gov/school_finance/index.shtml

CHAPTER 4

THE ACHIEVEMENT GAP FOR ENGLISH LANGUAGE LEARNERS

The Law, the Challenges, and a Possible Solution

Philip T. K. Daniel and Jeffrey C. Sun

OVERVIEW

Education policies are intended to address societal needs while affording a certain degree of discretion to educators who maintain specialized expertise. Today's modern school administrators face a variety of challenges in carrying out these education policies, a significant one being the task of providing effective instruction to an ever-growing group of English language learners (ELLs).[1] ELLs are children "whose difficulties in speaking, reading, writing, or understanding the English language may be sufficient to deny the individual . . . the ability to successfully achieve in classrooms where the language of instruction is English" (No Child Left Behind Act, 2014). ELLs are sometimes referred to as those with limited English

Law and Education Inequality, pages 49–59

school leaders face a great challenge in increasing student achievement scores of ELL students. These troubling statistics permeate even the most progressive schools with high ELL student populations undergoing active reform (DOE, 2014). A recent evaluation of schools participating in turnaround efforts through the federal School Improvement Grants program reported that while these progressive schools offered specialized supports for ELL students, only "moderate to limited attention to the unique needs" of ELL students during the initial phase of the turnaround process was recognized (DOE, 2014, p. 1).

In considering these data and the corresponding discrepancy between non-ELL and ELL students, it is important to understand the practical effects education policies may have on both students and administrators alike. Although education equity is indeed the ultimate goal, the use of school leader evaluations based on student performance (without taking into account the aforementioned demographic shifts) presents a significant hurdle for principals and other school leaders with high populations of ELL students. An unintended consequence may be disincentivizing or discouraging good school leaders from staying in schools with high ELL populations or pushing students to achieve certain measurable outcomes while forsaking a meaningful educational experience.

THE EQUAL EDUCATIONAL OPPORTUNITIES ACT AND "APPROPRIATE ACTION"

The Equal Educational Opportunities Act (EEOA) aims to protect certain populations of students who face language barriers (e.g., ELL students) from receiving unequal access to instructional programs. The EEOA (2014) states, "No State shall deny equal educational opportunity to an individual on account of his or her race, color, sex, or national origin." This denial includes "the failure by an educational agency to take appropriate action to overcome language barriers that impede equal participation by its students in its instructional programs" (2014).

In 1974, the U.S. Supreme Court had occasion to address and interpret this language barrier provision in the landmark case of *Lau v. Nichols*. In *Lau*, the Court ruled that the subject school had not provided non-English-speaking Chinese students with an equal educational opportunity to learn English as provided under the law. As the Court explained, the school district failed to establish "equality of treatment" (p. 556). Specifically, the Court criticized the school district's effort, noting that that equality is more than "providing students with the same facilities, textbooks, teachers, and curriculum"; the Court instead recognized that even with these provisions, "students who do not understand English are effectively foreclosed from any meaningful education" (p. 556). The Court continued that language essentially forms the basis for any meaningful education experience:

> Basic English skills are at the very core of what these public schools teach. Imposition of a requirement that, before a child can effectively participate in the educational program, he must already have acquired those basic skills is to make a mockery of public education. We know that those who do not understand English are certain to find their classroom experiences wholly incomprehensible and in no way meaningful. (p. 556)

Later that year, Congress responded to the *Lau* decision by enacting subsection (f) of the Bilingual Education Act (1974) so as to expressly include a responsibility to "remove language... barriers" that impede "true equality of educational opportunity" (1972, p. 6). The new provision within the Equal Educational Opportunities Act stated that denial of an equal educational opportunity may occur through "the failure by an educational agency to take appropriate action to overcome language barriers that impede equal participation by its students in its instructional programs." (Equal Educational Opportunities Act, 2014). This subsection is today widely known as the infamous "appropriate action" clause (Baker & de Kanter, 1983). Of course, that begs the question of what constitutes an "appropriate action?"

Potentially, the most helpful case in delineating appropriate action emerged from a federal circuit court in 1981. In *Castañeda v. Pickard,* the federal Court of Appeals for the Fifth Circuit offered guidance as to the definition of "appropriate" in the context of subsection (f)'s "appropriate action" clause. The *Castañeda* court offered a three-part inquiry to determine whether the school district's educational programming satisfied appropriate action. First it must "ascertain whether the school system is pursuing a program informed by an educational theory recognized as sound by some experts in the field or, at least, deemed a legitimate experimental strategy" (Castañeda v. Pickard, 1981, p. 1009). Second, it must examine "whether the programs and practices actually used by a school system are reasonably calculated to implement effectively the educational theory adopted by the school" (Castaneda v. Pickard, 1981, p. 1010).[5] Finally, courts must consider whether "a school system has adopted a sound program for alleviating the language barriers impeding the educational progress of some of its students and made bona fide efforts to make the program work does not necessarily end the court's inquiry into the appropriateness of the system's actions" (Castañeda v. Pickard, 1981, p. 1010).

In essence, *Castañeda* construed

> the statutory word "appropriate" so as to recognize both the obligation to take account of "the need of limited English speaking children for language assistance" and the fact that the "governance" of primary and secondary edu-

> cation ordinarily "is properly reserved to... state and local educational agencies." (Horne v. Flores, 2009, citing Castañeda v. Pickard, 1981, at 1008, 1009)

Succinctly stated, the overall inquiry centers on whether the students' language barriers have been overcome.

LEGAL/POLICY OBSTACLES TO ADVANCING STUDENT LEARNING

While schools are obligated to assist students in overcoming language barriers to ensure that every student can "participate meaningfully" in the programs each school district offers as indicated in the *Lau v. Nichols* case (1974), schools face several issues in doing so. First, administrators lack any straightforward direction or guidance from the federal government in implementing federal law and policy. Second, educators must acknowledge the uneven starting point at which ELLs and English-proficient students begin school. Finally, administrators are awarded only a finite (and often deficient) amount of resources, particularly in the areas of teacher training and experience, to remedy the disparities among ELL and English-proficient students. This chapter will address each of these issues in turn.

Lack of Meaningful Guidance

First, the federal government does not set out specific policies for schools to follow in designing and implementing ELL instructional programs, nor does it set guidelines for identifying or assessing ELL students (Calderón et al., 2011; Li, 2007; Myhill, 2004). Instead, these policies vary from state to state in the way ELL students are initially identified and assessed, and the way instructional programs for ELLs are shaped (Calderón et al., 2011).[6] The practical effect of this lack of guidance leaves states and local school districts without direction, resulting in serious educational disparities and a lack of any uniformity among school districts.

A prime example of how the federal government's ambiguous mandates lead to confusion in implementation is the case of *Horne v. Flores* (2009). In *Horne*, ELL students and parents sued Arizona for the state's failure to overcome language barriers, citing a lack of financial support for ELL programs as a primary reason for the deficiency. Although the case was filed in 1992, the Supreme Court did not provide a decision until 2009, ruling that financial support is only one of many factors a court should consider in evaluating a school's compliance with the EEOA. Specifically, in a contested 5–4 decision, the Court remanded the case to the district court to examine whether the facts demonstrated an "appropriate action." The Court indicated that district court judges must consider a variety of "important factual and legal changes" that may have affected the appropriateness of the school's action, that is, "the State's adoption of a new ELL instructional methodology, Congress' enactment of NCLB, structural and management reforms in [the contested school district], and increased overall education funding" (Horne v. Flores, 2009, p. 459). In so holding, the Court emphasized that student learning did not always directly correlate to a calculation of dollars spent. On the other hand, the dissent in *Horne* presented a lengthy discussion on how, notwithstanding the adoption of new programs, the students in the district at issue had low achievement scores. The dissent also argued that evidence had been presented documenting inadequate funding as the principle hurdle. The many factors relied upon by the Court in *Horne*—several of them ambiguously and broadly worded—reflect the challenge school leaders face in attempting to discern what constitutes "appropriate action."

Staggered Starting Line

Not only do schools have to concern themselves with taking affirmative action in the future, they must also be cognizant of the overall impediments ELLs face from the beginning. Otherwise stated, ELLs start public school at a disadvantage: in addition to learning the same subject matter as their English-proficient peers, they must also learn or improve their English. Moreover, school administrators face a large quantum of data showing that English language learners lag behind English-proficient children in many academic subjects. For example, English-speaking students outperform ELLs on state and national assessments, displaying a significant achievement gap between ELLs and English-proficient students (Echevarria, 2006).

The U.S. Department of Education conducted a study (The Early Childhood Longitudinal Study, or ECLS-K) tracking the academic performance of a nationally representative sample of language-minority students as compared to their English-proficient peers from kindergarten through eighth grade, starting from when the children were in kindergarten in 1998–1999 (DOE, 2012). The study found that "students whose primary home language was English and English Proficient students had higher overall mean eighth-grade (spring 2007) scores than did ELLs" (DOE, 2012, p. 2). Specifically, English and English-proficient students achieved higher overall scores than their language-minority counterparts in the subjects of reading and mathematics. The study also found that those children who "entered kindergarten proficient in English, regardless of their home language, scored higher on the ECLS-K eighth-grade reading, math, and science assessments

4. Researchers such as Dylan Conger (2013) point out that one's grade placement may assist in ELLs' academic progression. Specifically, it involves placing the student in the lower of the two possible grade placements. For instance, an ELL student who could fall within grades 9 or 10 would be placed in grade 9. Conger reveals, however, that the achievement only helps with math scores and it may be a temporary gain. Thus, as a solution, it is not a sufficient one.
5. The Court qualified this statement, indicating, "We do not believe that it may fairly be said that a school system is taking appropriate action to remedy language barriers if, despite the adoption of a promising theory, the system fails to follow through with practices, resources and personnel necessary to transform the theory into reality" (Castañeda v. Pickard, 1981, p. 1010).
6. The Council of Chief State School Officers has recently issued a document in an effort to standardize language and approaches to supporting ELLs (Linquanti & Cook, 2013).

REFERENCES

Baker, K. A., & de Kanter, A. A. (1983). Federal policy and the effectiveness of bilingual education. In K. A. Baker & A. A. de Kanter (Eds.), *Bilingual education: A reappraisal of federal policy* (pp. 33–86). Lexington, MA: Lexington.

Batalova, J., & McHugh, M. (2010). *Number and growth of students in U.S. schools in need of English instruction.* Washington, DC: Migration Policy Institute.

Bilingual Education Act, H.R.Rep. No. 92–1335, p. 6 (1972).

Bilingual Education Act, Pub. L. No. 93-380, § 105, 88 Stat. 484, 503–04 (1974).

Calderón, M., Slavin, R., & Sánchez, M. (2011). Effective instruction for English learners. *The Future of Children, 21*(1), 103–127.

Castañeda v. Pickard, 648 F.2d 989 (5th Cir. 1981).

Conger, D. (2013). The effect of grade placement on English language learners' academic achievement. *Educational Evaluation and Policy Analysis, 35*(4), 395–412.

Cooper, D., & Costa, K. (2012, June 1). Increasing the effectiveness and efficiency of existing public investments in early childhood education: Recommendations to boost program outcomes and efficiency. *Center for American Progress.* Retrieved from https://www.americanprogress.org/issues/education/report/2012/06/01/11723/increasing-the-effectiveness-and-efficiency-of-existing-public-investments-in-early-childhood-education/

Echevarria, J. (2006, February). *Helping English language learners succeed. Principal Leadership,* 16–21. Retrieved from https://www.nassp.org/portals/0/content/53392.pdf

Echevarria, J., Powers, K., & Elliott, J. (2004). Promising practices for curbing disproportionate representation of minority students in special education. *Issues in Teacher Education, 13*(1), 19–34.

Equal Educational Opportunities Act, 20 U.S.C. § 1703(f) (2014).

Horne v. Flores, 557 U.S. 433 (2009)

Lau v. Nichols, 414 U.S. 563 (1974)

Lhamon, C. E., Rosenfelt, P. H., & Samuels, J. (2014, May 8). *Dear Colleague letter: School enrollment procedures* [Dear Colleague letter from the U.S. Department of Justice and U.S. Department of Education]. Retrieved from http://www.justice.gov/crt/about/edu/documents/plylerletter.pdf

Li, B. (2007). From bilingual education to OELALEAALEPS: How the No Child Left Behind Act has undermined English language leaners' access to a meaningful education. *Georgetown Journal on Poverty Law & Policy, 14*(3), 539–572.

Linquanti, R., & Cook, H. G. (2013). *Toward a "common definition of English learner": Guidance for states and state assessment consortia in defining and addressing policy and technical issues and options.* Washington, DC: Council of Chief State School Officers.

Myhill, W. N. (2004). *The state of public education and the needs of English language learners in the era of "No Child Left Behind." Journal of Gender, Race & Justice, 8*(2), 393–447.

No Child Left Behind Act, 20 U.S.C. § 7801(25)(C)(i)(D)(i) (2014) (referring to the "Limited English Proficient" definition).

Ortiz, A., & Artiles, A. J. (2010). Meeting the needs of ELLs with disabilities: A linguistically and culturally responsive model. In G. Li & P. A. Edwards (Eds.), *Best practices in ELL instruction* (pp. 247–272). New York, NY: Guilford.

Rebell, M. A. (2012). The right to comprehensive education opportunity. *Harvard Civil Rights-Civil Liberties Law Review, 47*(1), 47–117.

Ruiz-de-Velasco, J., Fix, M., & Clewell, B. C. (2000). *Overlooked and underserved: Immigrant students in U.S. secondary schools.* Washington, DC: Urban Institute.

Tung, R. (2013). Innovations in educational equity for English language learners. *Voices in Urban Education, Summer, 2013*(37), 2–5.

U.S. Department of Education (DOE). (2002). Common core of data: Information on public schools and school districts in the United States. *National Center for Education Statistics.* Retrieved from http://nces.ed.gov/ccd

U.S. Department of Education (DOE). (2011, May). The condition of education 2011. *National Center for Education Statistics.* Retrieved from http://nces.ed.gov/pubs2011/2011033.pdf

U.S. Department of Education (DOE). (2012, April). Reading, mathematics, and science achievement of language-minority students in grade 8. *National Center for Education Statistics.* Retrieved from http://nces.ed.gov/pubs2012/2012028.pdf

U.S. Department of Education (DOE). (2013). The condition of education. *National Center for Education Statistics.* Retrieved from http://nces.ed.gov/programs/coe/

U.S. Department of Education (DOE). (2014). A focused look at schools receiving school improvement grants that have percentages of English language learner students. *Institute of Education Sciences.* Retrieved from http://ies.ed.gov/ncee/pubs/20144014/pdf/20144014.pdf

PART III

STUDENTS WITH DISABILITIES

rare. But she was kind and wanted to put my mind at ease, so she ordered a blood test. Two weeks later, the phone rang. It was the doctor. I stood beside my husband as he took the call and I heard him say, "Uh huh.... Okay, so corn, wheat, soy, fish, shellfish, peanuts, milk, and eggs."

> To this day, that memory brings back emotions that are difficult to put into writing. I knew our life had just changed in a way that I could not comprehend. I sat down with David and told him what the doctor had said. David's response made me smile. He said with all the wisdom of a 3-year old, "So that is what is making me sick. Oh good, then I just won't eat those foods." (B. Martinez, personal communication, November 12, 2011)

Fast forward five years and David is an 8 year old whose allergies have caused him to miss normal childhood activities such as Saturday afternoon birthday parties at a local restaurant and soccer team celebrations at the ice cream shop. In school, David is required to eat his lunch at a separate table designated the "peanut-free table" and outside his classroom, a poster signifies that his classroom is "peanut free." Additionally, David's mom receives hurtful glances and accusations from parents who believe the school's accommodations to David's peanut allergy are an inconvenience for the other students and their families.

Statistically, as many as three million American children under the age of 18 have food allergies, and each year approximately 50,000 children with allergies seek medical treatment in hospital emergency rooms (Dillon, 2011). A 2013 report from the Centers for Disease Control and Prevention indicates there was a 50% increase in the number of children with allergies since the late 1990s (as cited in Sicherer & Mahr, 2010). Additionally, Green and colleagues (2007) noted that between 1997 and 2007 the number of reported peanut allergies doubled and that the increase in food allergies (particularly peanut allergies) had risen to a level where 1 in every 20 school-aged children, approximately 1 child per classroom, was likely to have a food allergy.

With the number of food allergies on the rise (Laliberte, 2011), it becomes increasingly necessary for school districts to work toward an understanding of allergies, to recognize the school's role in providing a safe environment, and to develop guidelines and policy regarding allergy-related emergencies. This chapter provides information pertinent to school districts' legal responsibilities for children with allergies.

UNDERSTANDING AND MANAGING ALLERGIC REACTIONS

When an allergen is introduced into the system of a person with allergies, the body is unable to discern the difference between allergens and harmful toxins, and as a result the body, in essence, attacks itself. These attacks manifest in reactions that range in severity from itchy eyes to anaphylaxis, a "serious allergic response that often involves swelling, hives, lowered blood pressure and in severe cases, shock. If anaphylactic shock isn't treated immediately, it can be fatal" (AAAAI, n.d., para. 1).

There are multiple ways an allergen can trigger a reaction. The first and most common path involves ingestion. Children with ingestion allergies must consume the allergen and the allergen must enter the digestive tract in order to cause concern. Thus, children with ingestion allergies may be present at a classroom party where other children are eating peanut butter cookies as long as they do not ingest the cookies.

A second path whereby allergens may trigger allergic reactions is through touch. With this level of allergen sensitivity, children with, say, a peanut allergy, could be present at a classroom party where other children are eating peanut butter cookies as long as the child did not ingest or touch a surface that had come into contact with the peanut allergen. On its face, this allergen path appears fairly easy to monitor, but in actuality, this level of allergen sensitivity can be difficult to monitor when something as simple as a child who ate a peanut butter cookie touches the water faucet handle which is later touched by the student with the peanut allergy. The fact that the allergen transferred from the hands of the first child to the faucet handle may be sufficient transference for the child with a touch allergy to experience an allergic reaction.

The third allergen path is through inhalation. At this level of sensitivity, the child only need breathe the air where the allergen is present. So, say for example, if one child ate a peanut butter cookie at lunch and then whispered a secret to the child with a peanut allergy during recess, it is possible the airborne allergens would be sufficient to cause an allergic reaction in the child with the allergy.

However, there is no direct correlation between the path by which the allergen enters the body and the expected severity of the allergic reaction. For example, a child with touch allergies may come into physical contact with an allergen and suffer a minor rash, whereas another child may touch an allergen and suffer full anaphylactic shock. Thus, the manner in which the allergen enters the human body is not a direct indicator of the severity of the reaction that may occur (Young, 2006).

Currently, there are several philosophies that serve as the basis for plans to manage and reduce the severity of allergic reactions while children are in the school environment. Based on the work of the Asthmatic Schoolchildren's Treatment and Health Management Act of 2004, all 50 states have laws commonly referred to as "self-carry" or "self-administer" laws (Allergy and Asthma Network, n.d.), which allow students with life-threatening illnesses, who are of an appropriate age and maturity, to carry emergency medication (such as epinephrine for allergies or an inhaler for asthma) on their person. The assumption is that the proximity of the medication to the child will reduce the length of time to locate and subsequently administer the epinephrine. According to the National Institute of Health (NIH), however, physicians and school districts must carefully weigh the pros and cons of allowing individual students to self-carry medications as lost or misplaced medications could significantly increase the time between the intake of the allergen and the administration of the epinephrine (NIH, 2005).

Likewise, allowing students with allergies to "self-carry" is insufficient to protect all students with allergies. According to Sicherer and Mahr (2010), some 25% of the allergic reactions that occur during the school day involve students who have not been diagnosed with an allergy. To remediate the lack of epinephrine available for the 25% of undiagnosed students, Sicherer and Mahr suggest school districts maintain a prescription of epinephrine on site as "unassigned epinephrine for general use" (p. 1234). In 2013, Michigan addressed the matter of undiagnosed children with allergies and passed legislation that allows doctors to prescribe unassigned epinephrine to school boards (State of Michigan, 2013) thus ensuring children with unidentified allergies have access to epinephrine in Michigan schools.

Eggert (2013) suggests that relying on the presence of a school nurse to administer the epinephrine is unpredictable, especially in schools where nursing services are not available on a day-to-day basis or, as is the case in Michigan, where the school nurse-to-student ratio is one nurse for every 4,410 students. In an effort to reduce the time between allergic onset and the administration of medication, New Jersey passed legislation allowing individuals other than the school nurse to administer epinephrine (New Jersey Department of Education, 2008).

In states that permit schools to rely on persons other than school nurses to administer epinephrine, the schools are required to comprehensively train all or selected staff members in the administration of epinephrine so that they become proficient in the actions needed in an emergency situation and learn to recognize the symptoms of an allergic reaction (Hoff & Mitchell, 2010). For example, Michigan's newly passed legislation requires schools to have one to two persons trained in the use of the auto-injectors (State of Michigan, 2013), thus reducing reliance on the presence of school nurses or other medical personnel.

LEGAL PARAMETERS

Federal protections such as Section 504 of the Rehabilitation Act of 1974, the Americans with Disabilities Act (ADA) of 2008, the FDA Food Safety Modernization Act of 2011, the Health Insurance Portability and Accountability

Act (1996), and the United States Department of Agriculture guidelines address the rights of children with food allergies in the school environment. The legal protections discussed in the following sections are divided into two groups: legal parameters designed to protect persons with allergies and legal parameters pertinent to educational and medical records.

Legal Protections for Children With Allergies

Critical to both Section 504 and the ADA is the determination as to whether a child with an allergy meets the requirements to qualify as a disabled person. For protection under Section 504, a person must have a physical or mental impairment that substantially limits one or more major life activities, have a record of having such an impairment, or be regarded as having such an impairment (Rehabilitation Act, 1973). In determining whether a child with an allergy qualifies as a disabled person under Section 504, Plicka (1999) noted that entitlement to Section 504 protection is based on the severity of the allergic reaction and not on the fact that a diagnosis/impairment has a name. Munoz-Furlong (n.d.) wrote that children with allergies would meet the "legal definition of a 'disability' or 'handicap' where [the] physical impairment substantially limits one or more major life activities; such as eating or breathing."

Therefore, it is not that a child has an ingestion, touch, or inhalation allergy that qualifies the child for Section 504 protections. Rather, it is the severity in which the allergic reaction manifests itself. Ergo, itchy eyes and a runny nose do not constitute limitations of a major life activity and therefore are not likely to qualify a child with allergies as disabled under Section 504. However, a child whose reaction to allergens poses the strong possibility of an anaphylactic response may meet the legal definition of disability. Thus, the determining factor as to whether a child with allergies is protected under Section 504 or under ADA is not that the child has an allergy, rather the severity of the allergic reaction should one occur.

This quandary as to whether an allergy is sufficiently severe to merit ADA protection was altered in 2008 when the ADA was reauthorized and the new iteration included protections for inactive disabilities and disabilities in remission. The 2008 reauthorization, in essence, made it easier for persons with severe food allergies to qualify as a disabled person entitled to ADA and or Section 504 protection (Illinois State Board of Education and Illinois Department of Public Health, 2010).

In addition to legislation such as Section 504 and the ADA, students with allergies are also protected from discrimination by some less well-known legislation. For example, in 2011 the U.S. Congress passed the Food Safety Modernization Act (FSMA). Subsection 112 of the FSMA, known as the

Privacy Act (FERPA), also known as the Buckley Amendment, was enacted in 1974 to ensure that parents and students have access to their educational records. FERPA also requires that before an educational agency may release personally identifiable information to third parties, the parent (or eligible student) must provide signed and dated permission for the school to release or convey the information, including medical documents (FERPA, 1974). Failure to comply with FERPA's privacy provisions may result in a loss of federal funds (Klein, 2007).

A second piece of legislation that many would perceive as relevant to the gathering and sharing of medical information for students with allergies is the Health Insurance Portability and Accountability Act (HIPPA), which is designed to protect all "individually identifiable health information held or transmitted by a covered entity or its business associate, in any form or media, whether electronic, paper, or oral" (HIPPA, 1996, p. 3). This individually identifiable health information includes an "individual's past, present, or future physical or mental health or condition and the past, present, or future payment for the provision of health care to the individual" (p. 4). However, even though schools maintain and transmit student health records that may meet the definition of identifiable health information, as a rule public schools are not considered HIPPA-covered entities as student records (including health records) are deemed educational records and therefore fall under the protections of FERPA. According to the U.S. Department of Health & Human Services (n.d.), "While schools and school districts maintain student health records, these records are in most cases protected by the Family Educational Rights and Privacy Act (FERPA) and not HIPAA" (para. 3).

CONCLUSION

There are more than three million children with food allergies. Statistically, that equates to approximately one child in each U.S. public school classroom. Whether the allergic reactions manifest from ingesting, touching, or inhaling the allergen, allergic reactions can be serious medical events that may lead to anaphylaxis and death. Due to the large number of children with allergies, it is prudent for schools to take action to reduce the number and severity of allergic reactions. To date, there are multiple measures in use to reduce serious effects from allergic episodes that occur during the school day.

First, all 50 states have self-carry/self-administer laws which allow students (who are physically and mentally able) to carry medication such as epinephrine on their person. Also, several states have (or are in the process of passing) laws that will allow doctors to write prescriptions directly to a school district which will mean epinephrine would be available for use by any student in need of the medication. Additionally, some states are passing laws that permit individuals other than medical personnel to be trained in the administration of epinephrine.

Additionally, there are laws such as Section 504 and ADA that provide protection from discrimination once it is determined the child's allergies constitute a legal disability. Upon learning that a child has an allergy, the school district should apply allergen restrictions that are commensurate with the child's allergy. For example, it may not be an appropriate decision to make an entire school building peanut free just because one child develops a minor rash if she eats peanut butter.

The FSMA and the USDA guidelines provide protections for children with allergies from unnecessary segregation in common eating areas and assure that children can receive an allergen-free meal. Additionally, it is likely student health records will be deemed educational records and will be protected under FERPA rather than HIPPA. The legal parameters discussed in this chapter create an umbrella of protection for students with life-threatening allergies. Additionally, there are multiple organizations (see Appendix) designed to keep parents and educators informed of legal updates and current medical practices.

APPENDIX
Professional and Nonprofit Allergy Organizations

Food Allergy Research & Education (FARE): The Food Allergy Research & Education (FARE) formed in 2012 when the Food Allergy & Anaphylaxis Network (FAAN) merged with the Food Allergy Initiative (FAI). This merger brought together the expertise and leadership of FAAN, "the most trusted source of food allergy information, programs, and resources" (FARE, para. 1) with the extensive funding and private research support of FAI. As the leading food allergy organization, FARE works on behalf of individuals with food allergies and those who are at risk of suffering from life-threatening anaphylaxis.

FARE National Headquarters
7925 Jones Branch Drive
Suite 1100
McLean, VA 22102
Toll-Free: 1-800-929-4040
Main: 703-691-3179
Fax: 703-691-2713

Kids With Food Allergies (KFA): The Kids with Food Allergies organization has over 24,000 members. A not-for-profit organization, KFA provides several areas of support for parents of children with allergies and other individuals and loved ones that want to learn more about caring for people with allergies. The KFA website offers help with current news and information regarding allergies, recipes, food recalls, support forums, and guideline resources.

Kids with Food Allergies
73 Old Dublin Pike, Ste 10, #163
Doylestown, PA 18901
Office Line: (215) 230-5394
Fax: (215) 340-7674
http://www.kidswithfoodallergies.org/

The Allergic Child: The Allergic Child organization was founded by parents of a child that was diagnosed with a severe food allergy. Their experiences and knowledge aim to help other parents learn to live with such a serious medical condition. The website created by this organization includes numerous resources such as current legislation as well as the history of allergy legislation throughout the United States. In addition, the website shares information about current "allergy aware" schools that members have described from experiences and children's stories, schools that help young children with or without allergies come to learn more about the allergy diagnosis.

AllergicChild.com
425 W Rockrimmon Blvd
Suite 202
Colorado Springs, CO 80919
http://www.allergicchild.com/

American Academy of Allergy Asthma & Immunology (AAAAI): The American Academy of Allergy Asthma and Immunology is a professional organization composed of healthcare professionals who specialize in asthma, immunology, and allergies. With its 6,500 members and 16 board members, the AAAAI stretches across the United States, Canada, and 60 other countries. The AAAAI contributes to the medical field with its contributions to fund medical research and education, and through a monthly journal that has been recognized as being the most cited journal in the United States that is devoted to allergy/immunology.

American Academy of Allergy, Asthma and Immunology (AAAAI)
555 East Wells Stree
Suite 1100
Milwaukee, WI 53202-3823
414-272-6071
http://www.aaaai.org
http://www.aaaai.org/patients/resources/fact_sheets/food_allergy.pdf
http://www.aaaai.org/members/allied_health/tool_kit/ppt/

CHAPTER 6

THE IDEA TRANSITION

Individualizing Educational Opportunities for Students With Disabilities

Susan C. Bon and Nicole D. Snyder

Historically, the postschool outcomes for students with disabilities reveals significant disparities in terms of employment and postsecondary education (Wagner, Newman, Cameto, Garza, & Levine, 2005). A comparison of the National Longitudinal Transition Study 1 (NLTS1) from the mid-1980s to the National Longitudinal Transition Study 2 (NLTS2) in 2003, how ever, shows significant increases in positive post-high school outcomes for students with disabilities. For example, in 1990, only 26% of students with disabilities enrolled in two- or four-year colleges, but in 2005, this increased to 46% enrollment (NCSER, 2010). Conversely, students with disabilities continue to experience higher rates of unemployment and underemployment than their peers without disabilities, with the exception reported for students from high-income families who experienced a significant increase in employment rate (Newman et al., 2011, DOL, BLS, 2011).

Law and Education Inequality, pages 77–93

Although the data from the most recent National Longitudinal Transition Study (IES, 2012) has not yet been released and may provide evidence of continued gains, students with disabilities are expected to encounter many challenges as they transition from secondary to postsecondary environments. Further, there is an increasing number of students who are identified with an autism spectrum disorder (CDC, 2014). These students will eventually be transitioning into postsecondary settings. Thus, it is likely that an increased number of students will be in need of effective transitions services and programs that support access to higher education insititutions as well as employment opportunities. In an effort to remove barriers to educational opportuities, it is especially important for educators and all school leaders to be keenly aware of not only the legal mandates but also the evidence-based practices that could support successful transitions for students with disabilities.

With respect to the legal mandate, the Individuals with Disabilities in Education Act of 2004 (IDEA) provides a statutory framework for local education agencies (LEAs), which mandates the provision of transition planning and services for students with disabilities entering postsecondary employment and education programs. While the the IDEA does not specifically implicate evidence-based practices with respect to transition planning, there is growing interest and support for including these practices in an effort to promote successful transitions for students with disabilities (Prince, Katsiyannis, & Farmer, 2013). Although the purpose of this chapter is to provide an overview and update on legal developments, specifically statutory and judicial updates, the chapter also will briefly address the practices that emerge from the professional literature as well as evidence-based research.

This chapter will first provide an overview of the IDEA with specific focus on transition planning and services requirements, as well as the implementation of federal regulations. Next, the chapter briefly reviews earlier transition cases and then provides an analysis and summary of cases emerging from the courts since the 2004 reauthorization of the IDEA. Finally, the chapter concludes with implications and suggestions for schools and school leaders who are responsible for providing pathways of transition between secondary and postsecondary environments, and for helping students with disabilities overcome the challenges and barriers faced in higher education institutions.

OVERVIEW OF THE IDEA TRANSITION PLAN REQUIREMENTS

In 1983, Congress introduced transition services as a special education concept by authorizing federal funding for states "to assist in the transitional process to postsecondary education, vocational training, competitive employment, continuing education, or adult services" (Education of the Handicapped Act, 1983). However, Congress did not require states to supply transition services at this time. Transition planning was later introduced as a mandate for services when the Act's name was changed to the Individuals with Disabilities Education Act (1990).

According to the 1990 amendments, transition services that focus on postschool outcomes should be provided to all students with disabilities. Specifically, students with disabilities should be provided with individualized education programs containing a "statement of the needed transition services for students beginning no later than age 16 and annually thereafter (and, when determined appropriate for the individual, beginning at age 14 or younger)" (IDEA, 1990). Congress also amended the definition of transition services in the IDEA (1990) to emphasize an outcome-oriented process, focus on individualized needs, and the promotion of a variety of postschool opportunities. Not long after these changes, the Individuals with Disabilities Act (1997) was amended to require a transition services statement of needs specific to the child's course of study. The 1997 amendments required the inclusion of this statement and transition planning to begin at age 14 and to be updated each year (§ 614(d)(1)(A)(vii)(I)).

The IDEA was again reauthorized in 2004 and included modest updates to the transition requirements for students with disabilities. Specifically, the IDEA now requires transition planning to be in effect when the child is 16 and to be updated annually. The transition plan must include postsecondary goals such as training, education, employment, and, independent living skills (where appropriate). In addition, the plan should identify transition services, such as courses of study, and notification of the child's rights upon reaching the age of majority (20 U.S.C. § 1414(d)(1)(A)(i)(VIII); 34 C.F.R. § 300.320(b)).

> Transition services are defined as a coordinated set of activities that
>
> (A) is designed to be within a results-oriented process, that is focused on improving the academic and functional achievement of the child with a disability to facilitate the child's movement from school to post-school activities, including post-secondary education, vocational education, integrated employment (including supported employment), continuing and adult education, adult services, independent living, or community participation;
>
> (B) is based on the individual child's needs, taking into account the child's strengths, preferences, and interests; and
>
> (C) includes instruction, related services, community experiences, the development of employment and other post-school adult living objectives, and, when appropriate, acquisition of daily living skills and functional vocational evaluation. (20 U.S.C. § 1401(34); 34 C.F.R. § 300.43(a))

Similarly, in *Pace v. Bogalusa City School Board* (2001), a student with cerebral palsy and multiple learning disabilities argued that the LEA did not provide any transition services to him. The court disagreed, noting that the school identified some state and local agencies that might have been able to assist the student and encouraged the student and his parents to contact the agencies directly in an attempt to determine if the student qualified for services through any of them. Even though the student may not have established contact with these agencies, the court determined that the school had fulfilled its obligations with regard to agency linkages.

Conversely, in *Yankton School District v. Schramm* (1995), the court concluded that pointing a student in the direction of outside agencies was not sufficient to comply with the IDEA requirement of linking a student with outside agencies. The court reasoned that Congress intended for local school districts to familiarize themselves with the various opportunities and services available to disabled students in their community and then make effective use of that information in transition planning (Ray, 2002).

In a 1996 case, the Tenth Circuit upheld the appropriateness of transition services despite failure to include them in an IEP. In *Urban v. Jefferson County School District* (1996), the student received services and educational experiences relating to his postschool activities, including job-site training. While his IEP did not set forth goals and objectives relating to transition, it included community-awareness services, daily living skills, and experiences to assist him in learning how to make store purchases. The court concluded that because the LEA's procedural violation of failing to include transition services in the IEP did not amount to a substantive deprivation, there was no violation of the student's right to an appropriate education.

While these earlier cases were measured predominantly against the *Rowley* two-prong standard, subsequent court decisions rely not only on the *Rowley* standard but also on the increased substantive and procedural FAPE requirements in the 2004 IDEA amendments. Yet the 2004 amendments to the IDEA did not modify the *Rowley* standard regarding FAPE, subsequently the courts have interpreted the IDEA regulations as not dictating a separate FAPE requirement for transition plans (Klein Independent School District v. Hovem, 2010). This has led, in part, to more complex issues before the courts than those that were faced by courts in early transition services cases.

When determining the provision and adequacy of transition plans and services, recent courts have generally recognized the appropriateness of transition services that are individualized, detailed, and that create opportunities for desired outcomes (Morse, Osborne, & Russo, 2008). Courts have similarly recognized that the IDEA does not guarantee specific results and that local education agencies (LEAs) are not required to ensure that a student is successful in fulfilling all desired goals (K.C. ex rel. Her Parents v. Nazareth Area School District, 2011). However, courts find fault with LEAs when transition services are uncoordinated, generalized, broad, or abstract (Klein Independent School District v. Hovem, 2010).

Although federal courts have provided guidance with respect to transition planning and services, their interpretations of the IDEA mandates have varied. The recent cases discussed below provide additional clarity regarding the IDEA mandated transition services and programs that schools and school leaders are obligated to provide to students with disabilities. We first identify cases in which school districts met the required the IDEA transition planning services, and then examine those instances in which the courts found that student rights were violated as a result of schools' failure to provide the required transition services.

Substantive Versus Procedural Defects

Courts have held that although the IDEA requires IEPs to contain statements of transition services, neither section requires that those statements be articulated in a separate component of the IEP; thus, merely pointing to the absence of a stand-alone transition plan is insufficient to form the basis for a founded claim of procedural error (Lessard v. Wilton-Lyndeborough Cooperative School District, 2008). Furthermore, even when transition planning and services were inadequate, courts have held that such inadequacies were procedural flaws that did not amount to denials of FAPE.

For example, the Third Circuit upheld a New Jersey district court decision that an IEP team's failure to adequately discuss and describe transition needs and services did not violate the student's substantive FAPE rights (Rodrigues v. Fort Lee Board of Education, 2011). In fact, the student's IEP identified her plan to attend college as well the academic requirements that were necessary to prepare for college. She also received extensive support and related services aimed at self-advocacy and independent skills. Finally, the court relied squarely on the Seventh Circuit's ruling that the failure to adequately describe transition services is a procedural violation (Board of Education v. Ross, 2007).

Relying on the *Rowley* standard, two district courts in Pennsylvania noted that the IDEA creates opportunities but does not guarantee specific results (Coleman v. Pottstown, 2013; High v. Exeter Township School District, 2010). Both of the Pennsylvania courts also relied on this basic principle: "The floor set by IDEA for adequate transition services appears to be low, focusing on whether opportunities are created for a disabled student to pursue independent living and a career, not just a promise of a particular result" (K.C., 2011, at 822). Consequently, the focus is on whether opportunities are created for a disabled student to pursue independent living and a career, not just a promise of a particular result. In *Coleman v. Pottstown* (2013), the school system provided the student with exposure to and opportunities to access vocational services, courses in mechanics, computer training, and culinary arts. The IEP team further individualized the student's experiences by supporting his interest in a possible career path within the U.S. military. Similarly, the court rejected the parents' claim that the school system should provide progress monitoring of the transition goals in *High v. Exeter* (2010). According to the court, annual updates to the transition plan must include measurable goals and corresponding services, but not progress monitoring.

In one of the most recent cases, a California district court found that the inadequacies in transition services did not reach a FAPE violation (C.B. v. Garden Grove Unified School District, 2014). According to the court, the student has several years ahead of him in school and thus would still have an opportunity to meet individualized transition goals. Courts in Wisconsin and Massachussetts similarly upheld transition-service plans despite procedural defects. In the Wisconsin decision, the LEA was able to demonstrate on-the-job progress and the role of the IEP's transition services in making the student more employable and proficient in his life skills (Rosinksy v. Green Bay Area School Distric*t*, 2009). Likewise, the Massachussetts court determined that a "stand-alone" transition plan was not required in light of evidence that transition planning discussions were held at all of the student's IEP team meetings and transition services were, in fact, provided (Sebastian M. v. King Philip Regional School District, 2011).

Adequate Transition Services

Federal trial courts in Pennsylvania and Indiana have upheld transition plans and services when LEAs were able to show that they provided a coordinated set of transition activities which sufficiently met the FAPE standard. In Pennsylvania, the court explained that a parent cannot simply argue that an IEP is deficient because it fails to state how a student will meet a transition goal (K.C. ex rel. Her Parents v. Nazareth Area School District, 2011). There is no requirement for a transition plan to dictate IEP goals. Unlike the IEP, the court reasoned that a "transition plan is not a strictly academic plan, but related to several post-secondary skills, including independent living skills and employment" (K.C. ex rel. Her Parents v. Nazareth Area School District, 2011, 806 F. Supp., at 822). The LEA provided adequate travel training and helped the student make meaningful progress toward moving effectively and safely from place to place. Moreover, the team began discussing transition goals and needs in advance of evaluations and offered the student an opportunity to participate in relevant classes and community-based services. Finally, in this case, parental interference impeded attempts to provide a more individualized plan, and the LEA was not required to include all recommendations of the parents' expert.

In Indiana, a district court upheld the LEA's provision of transition services in a case involving a 19-year-old student with an autism spectrum disorder (Tindell v. Evansville-Vanderburgh School Corporaton, 2011). While the transition plan was procedurally lacking, the inadequacies did not deny the student a FAPE because, prior to the student's residential placement, no reasonable transition plan could be developed or implemented for him. Up to that point, the student's anxiety and mood disorder so severely impacted his ability and willingness to develop life skills appropriate for his age that he was not in a position to benefit from an in-depth transition plan providing advanced vocational or social skills. The student's IEPs uniformly demonstrated that the school provided adequate transition services as soon as the student was in a position to benefit from the adult-level educational and vocational support services.

Inadequate Transition Services

In a few circumstances, courts have found that students' FAPE rights were denied as a result of inadequate transition plans. Federal trial courts in Texas (Klein Independent School District v. Hovem, 2010), Massachusetts (Dracut School Community v. Bureau of Special Education, 2010), and Alabama (Jefferson County Board of Education v. Lolita S., 2013) held that inappropriate transition plans might deny a student's right to a FAPE. In these cases, the goals and services were not sufficiently individualized or clear, and failed to address the students' academic and functional achievement needs.

The district court in Texas determined that the student's transition plan was not individualized because it lacked results-oriented measurable goals as well as transition services to meet the student's needs after high school (Klein Independent School District v. Hovem, 2010). Moreover, the student never met with a guidance counselor about postschool transition planning. Although his plan contained a goal to pass his classes and graduate high school, the plan failed to address the student's handwriting and written expression needs, thus the student was unprepared in the most basic life skills in postschool settings. According to the Texas court, the IDEA requires measurable or results-oriented goals, which are designed to facilitate the transition from school to postsecondary opportunities.

The Massachusetts district court in *Dracut* determined that two distinct components of the student's transition plan were inadequate. First, the

postsecondary settings (Klein Independent School District v. Hovem, 2010). The emphasis on individualized transition services, plans, and goals is prevalent in the statutory framework and regulations (20 U.S.C. § 1401(34); 34 C.F.R. § 300.43(a)) as well as the case law (see e.g., Jefferson County Board of Education v. Lolita S., 2013). In *Jefferson*, the student's IEP merely identified common experiences for all entering freshman, which were focused on general vocational and career-based training. On the other hand, in at least one of the cases, the court ruled in favor of a school district that had developed individualized transition services and goals, even though there were procedural errors during the transition-planning process. The court recognized the school district's efforts to provide transition services and experiences that were unique to the student's interests in *Coleman v. Pottstown* (2013).

Despite the importance of providing individualized educational opportunities and recognizing unique learning needs of students with disabilities, researchers point to a countertrend as a result of standardized testing and the inclusion movement (Goodman, Hazelkorn, Bucholz, Duffy, & Kitta, 2011). As a result of the standardized testing and inclusive policy movements, Goodman and colleagues (2011) assert that students with disabilities have experienced decreases in graduation rates, which they further suggest may be related to a focus on the general curriculum at the expense of providing an individualized education based on the students' unique learning abilities and needs. Although not specifically focused on transition services, Goodman and colleagues identify the risks in general of moving away from individualized educational opportunities to generalized curriculums and testing for all students.

Given the critical role of the transition plans and services for preparing students for life after school, it is necessary to bridge any disconnect between K–12 schools and postsecondary programs. Through collaborative transition planning among educatonal institutions across the K–12 continuum, which is consistent with EBPs and legal mandates, the barriers to higher education may be overcome for students with disabilities. The following section breifly reviews the disconnect between K–12 schools and postsecondary settings and advocates for meaningful dialogue among school districts, educators, parents, and higher-education insititutions in an effort to help students with disabilities overcome the disconnect.

Understanding the Disconnect

The fragmented nature of education governance adds to the challenges that students with disabilities encounter when they transition from high school to postsecondary environments. While the IDEA governs students' rights and LEA responsibilities in secondary schools, the IDEA is no longer applicable in the postsecondary environment. Because transition plans are within the purview of the IDEA and the K–12 administrators, these plans are developed by members of the IEP team and included in a students' IEP. Ironically then, the plan, which is designed to address how the student with a disability will prepare for postsecondary education, is probably never seen by the postsecondary institution.

The transition from a K–12 environment to postsecondary institutions for students with disabilities is further complicated by the shift in applicable statutes as well as by the reduction in programs and services provided to students. Specifically, secondary students in the public school setting are treated as an IEP team member, but administrators and parents generally determine what accommodations will be necessary for the student. Yet once this same student enters higher education, the ADA requires that the student become her or his own advocate, register with the appropriate office, and self-disclose to professors the disability and reasonable accommodations. In order to successfully transition to a postsecondary setting, students with disabilities must learn to assume new responsibilities that they did not have in high school (Eckes & Ochoa, 2005) and how to navigate significantly different legal provisions and protections.

Although both the Americans with Disabilities Act Amendments (ADAA) of 2008 and the Rehabilitation Act of 1973 protect and govern access to postsecondary education for individuals with disabilities, these provisions offer far less extensive guaranteed services than what students are accustomed to under the IDEA. Under the ADAA and Rehabilitation Act, an individual with a documented disability (who is otherwise qualified) is only guaranteed equal access to educational opportunities in the higher education institution (Shaw, Keenan, Madaus, & Banerjee, 2010). Providing access to educational opportunities is markedly different from guaranteeing that a student with a disability is provided a FAPE, as required by the IDEA.

An increasing number of universities and colleges are making efforts to enroll students with disabilities in their institutions. One way to achieve this goal is through the adoption of streamlined and standardized documentation requirements and guidelines. Currently, college guidelines and requirements vary widely given the absence of clearly established definitions (DOE, OCR, 2011). Consequently, students and families, as well secondary personnel who identify students' needs and provide transition services, are at a great disadvantage and encounter uncertainty from institution to institution.

Additional requirements, including documentation of the disability, are often another challenge to students. Specifically, the Offices of Disability Services at universities are authorized to ask students to provide documentation that is no older than 3 years. Students with disabilities who may have been evaluated in early grades but not reevaluated during high school are unlikely to have the necessary records. In such circumstances, the expense to the child and family may be an impediment to receiving needed supports and services at the university level. Ultimately, school districts and higher-education institutions should work together to identify strategies that are directly aligned with the IDEA transition planning and services mandate and that reflect the changing legal landscape that faces students and their families upon enrollment in postsecondary institutions.

CONCLUSION

In response to this disjointed process of transitioning from K–12 to higher-education settings, disability researchers have emhpasized EBPs such as self-determination skills. Such interventions are essential to students with disabilities who may no longer have formal support or extensive services as they transition from secondary to postsecondary environments (Kuangparichat, 2010). Through self-determination, students take charge of their lives and are empowered to make decisions with minimal influence from outside sources. Further, students with self-determination skills are better equipped to develop problem-solving strategies and positive social beaviors that enhance interpersonal relationships (Alwell & Cobb, 2009).

Navigating the EBPs as well as the legal mandates will continue to pose challenges for school districts. School districts and educators are encouraged to adopt transition planning services and programs that provide students with educational benefit as well as individualized goals and opportunities. Specifically, school districts should develop a system to monitor the transition-services planning process first for legal compliance—provide educational benefit (*Rowley*) that is individualized to meet the student's unique needs—and then for EBPs, such as the development of self-determination and self-advocacy skills.

The provision of postsecondary disability services is both emergent and dynamic as a result of judicial intervention, best practices, and changing laws and policies. As students with disabilities enroll in greater numbers in postsecondary institutions, school districts will face increasing demands to provide meaningful transition-planning support to students and families who are struggling to overcome the significant disconnect between secondary and postsecondary institutions (Shaw et al., 2010).

REFERENCES

Alwell, M. & Cobb, B. (2009). Social and communicative interventions and transition outcomes for youth with disabilities. *Career Development for Exceptional Individuals, 32*, 94–107.

Americans with Disabilities Act Amendments Act of 2008, Pub. L. No. 110-325.

Board of Education v. Ross, 486 F.3d 267 (7th Cir. 2007).

Board of Education of the Hendrick Hudson Central School District v. Rowley, 458 U.S. 176 (1982).

Browell v. Lemahieu, 127 F. Supp. 2d 1117 (D. Haw. 2000).

Burns, M. K., & Ysseldyke, J. E. (2009). Reported prevalence of evidence-based instructional practices in special education. *Journal of Special Education, 43*(1), 3–11. doi: 10.1177/0022466908315563

C.B. v. Garden Grove Unified School District, 575 Fed. App'x. 796 (9th Cir. 2014)

Centers for Disease Control and Prevention (CDC). (2014, March 28). Prevalence of autism spectrum disorder among children aged 8 years—Autism and Developmental Disabilities Monitoring Network, 11 Sites, United States, 2010. *Morbidity and Mortality Weekly Report Surveillance Summaries, 63*(2), 1–21.

Coleman v. Pottstown Sch. Dist. (2013) 983 F.Supp.2d 543.

Dracut School Community v. Bureau of Special Education, 737 F. Supp. 2d 35 (D. Mass. 2010).

Eckes, S., & Ochoa, T. (2005). Students with disabilities: Transitioning from high school to higher education. *American Secondary Education, 33,* 6–18.

Education of the Handicapped Act Amendments of 1983. 20 U.S.C. § 1400.

Goodman, J. I., Hazelkorn, M., Bucholz, J. L., Duffy, M. L., & Kitta, Y. (2011). Inclusion and graduation rates: What are the outcomes? *Journal of Disability Policy Studies, 21,* 241–252.

Hadley, W. M., & Satterfield, J. W. (2013). Are university students with learning disabilities getting the help they need? *Journal of the First-Year Experience & Students in Transition, 25,* 113–124.

Hess, K. L., Morrier, M. J., Heflin, L. J., & Ivey, M. L. (2008). Autism treatment survey: Services received by children with autism spectrum disorders in public school classrooms. *Journal of Autism and Developmental Disorders, 38,* 961–971.

High v. Exeter Township School District, 2010 WL 363832 (E.D. Pa. 2010).

Individuals with Disabilities Education Act (IDEA) 20 U.S.C. § 1400 et seq. (1997).

Individuals with Disabilities Education Act (2004). Pub. L. No. 108-446, 118 Stat. 2647 (2004) (codified at 20 U.S.C. §§ 1400-1491).

Institute of Education Sciences (IES). (2012). *National Longitudinal Transition Study 2012.* Retrieved from http://ies.ed.gov/ncee/nlts/

Jefferson County Board of Education v. Lolita S., — F.Supp.2d —, 2013 WL 5519656 (N.D.Ala. 2013).

K.C. *ex rel.* Her Parents v. Nazareth Area School District, 806 F. Supp. 2d 806 (E.D. Pa. 2011).

Klein Independent School District v. Hovem, 745 F. Supp. 2d 700 (S.D. Tex. 2010).

Kuangparichat, M. (2010). Legal rights of young adults with autism: Transitioning into mainstream adulthood. *Widener Law Review, 16,* 175–206.

Lessard v. Wilton-Lyndeborough Cooperative School District, 518 F.3d 18 (1st Cir. 2008).

Mazzotti, V. L., & Plotner, A. J. (2014). Service providers implementing secondary transition evidence-based practices: A multi-state survey of transition. *Career Development and Transition for Exceptional Individuals.* doi: 10.1177/2165143414544360

PART IV

BULLYING AND LGBT YOUTH

CHAPTER 7

AN OVERVIEW OF JUDICIAL AND LEGISLATIVE RESPONSES TO THE BULLYING EPIDEMIC

Richard T. Geisel, Brenda R. Kallio, and Christa Brodina

Teasing and being teased may be normal parts of growing up, but bullying is not. Educators may be hard-pressed to differentiate between teasing and bullying, which have become increasingly common occurrences in childhood. Given the seemingly blurred lines between bullying and teasing, educators may "overact to normal teasing interactions between students or fail to react to incidents of true bullying" (Conn, 2004, p. 30). Since some examples of bullying may invoke the protections of state and federal antidiscrimination laws, and in some extreme scenarios basic constitutional rights, the appropriate recourse for victims may not be readily apparent.

For instance, in *Morrow v. Balaski* (2013), the court ruled that the school violated the student's Fourteenth Amendment due process rights when the student experienced bullying during the school day. Explaining the school's limited duty to protect students from private actors under the Due Process Clause, the federal district court granted summary judgment to the school district. The court noted, "The Due Process Clause is not a surrogate for local tort law or state statutory and administrative remedies; nor is substantive

Law and Education Inequality, pages 97–128

> where defendant's response was so inadequate or ineffective that discriminatory intent may be inferred. In other words, deliberate indifference requires a finding that the District's actions or inactions in response to known harassment effectively caused further harassment to occur. (Zeno, 2012, p. 669)

Citing numerous examples of the school district's failure to be more proactive, the Second Circuit asserted that a jury may reasonably determine the inadequacy or ineffectiveness of the school district's response to the bullying. Thus, the *Zeno* case illustrates that Title VI may provide a legal recourse for students who are bullied based on their race, color, or national origin. However, this only applies in cases where the bullying is severe, when it can be proven that the bullying is under the school district's control, the district has actual knowledge of the bullying, and when the district is deliberately indifferent to the bullying based on their actions or the lack thereof.

Discrimination Based on Sex: Title IX of the Education Amendments of 1972

Title IX of the Education Amendments (1972) is comprehensive federal legislation that prohibits federally funded education programs or activities from discriminating on the basis of sex. The seminal case, *Davis v. Monroe* (1999), established the peer-based sexual harassment standard under Title IX. In this case, a male elementary school student sexually harassed a 5th-grade female student by repeatedly attempting to touch her breasts and genitalia and making sexually aggressive and suggestive statements to her during class over a period of several months. Although the harassment was reported to school administrators, the harasser went undisciplined until he was finally charged with (and pleaded guilty to) sexual battery. When the female child's parent filed suit asserting violations of Title IX, lower courts ruled in favor of the school district on the basis that there was no private right of action under Title IX for peer-on-peer harassment. Nevertheless, on appeal to the U.S. Supreme Court, a divided Court did indeed recognize such a right under Title IX in extreme cases. Subsequently, the Court established that the liability standard for peer-on-peer harassment under Title IX is met where the district (a) responded with deliberate indifference, (b) had actual knowledge, (c) controlled the situation, and (d) there is evidence of severe, pervasive, and objectively offensive behavior that interferes with the plaintiff's educational opportunity. As many plaintiffs have discovered, the *Davis* standard is a difficult one to prove.

The sexual harassment alegations in *Davis* are strikingly similar to the conduct described as bullying in a number of recent cases. An example of such a case is *A. A. ex rel. Antle v. Portage Township Schools* (2013), in which several male students harassed a female by grabbing and squeezing her breasts and genitalia. Similar to *Davis*, the plaintiffs asserted the school district had a duty under Title IX to protect the student from bullying. Unlike *Davis*, however, the *Antle* court dismissed the Title IX claims due to the school's lack of knowledge regarding the bullying behaviors. Furthermore, the court found that the plaintiff failed to demonstrate "that she suffered a concrete, negative effect on her education as a result of the sexual harassment that occurred" (Antle, 2013, at 16). This case underscores how difficult it can be to successfully argue a deprivation of rights under Title IX, even for bullying that takes the form of sexual harassment.

When students are bullied based on their actual or perceived sexual orientation, the student may be protected by the sex discrimination guidelines recognized under Title IX. An area of bullying rooted in sexual harassment that is currently in a state of flux is bullying based on a student's actual or perceived sexual orientation. While lower federal courts (e.g., *Tyrrell v. Seaford Union Free School District*, 2011) have ruled that there is no cause of action under Title IX for peer harassment based on a student's actual or perceived sexual orientation, recent guidance from the U.S. Department of Education, Office of Civil Rights (2014) declares,

> Title IX's sex discrimination prohibition extends to claims of discrimination based on gender identity or failure to conform to stereotypical notions of masculinity or femininity and OCR accepts such complaints for investigation. Similarly, the actual or perceived sexual orientation or gender identity of the parties does not change a school's obligations. (p. 5)

While the Department's guidance may appear incongruent with current case law on the matter, it should be noted that lower courts did not recognize a private right of action under Title IX for peer harassment prior to *Davis*, yet school law attorneys were warning their clients ahead of time that such harassment left unchecked could present liability under Title IX. Whether courts eventually recognize such a right for harassment based on actual or perceived sexual orientation, it is important to note that *Davis* still presents a significant hurdle for any peer-on-peer sexual harassment case brought under Title IX.

Given the high burden established under Title IX for peer sexual harassment claims, students who seek to recover damages or relief for bullying pursuant to this federal law are unlikely to prevail. Specifically, in *Davis* (1999) the Court explicitly stated that "damages are not available for simple acts of teasing and name-calling among school children, even where these comments target differences in gender" (p. 652) (see http://mutex.gmu.edu:2083/universe/document?_m=aae1798596ea023af5039c2033372185&_docnum=70&wchp=dGLbVtb-zSkVA&_md5=c52b0156

a93ea6c29ffc71eb469c07ac-n62). As the following discussion of disability discrimination and related federal laws reveals, the courts have responded in a slightly different manner to harassment and bullying complaints by students with disabilities.

Discrimination Based on Disability

Similar to the specific protections under Title VI and Title IX, individuals with disabilities are protected from discrimination under federal law. Three federal statutes offer remedies and relief for discrimination based on disability: Section 504 of the Rehabilitation Act of 1973, the Americans with Disabilities Amendments Act (ADA, 2008), and the Individuals with Disabilities Education Act (IDEA, 2004).

Section 504 of the Rehabilitation Act of 1973 extends civil rights protection to persons with disabilities by including all the remedies, procedures, and rights contained in the Civil Rights Act of 1964. Additionally, Section 504 protects children with qualifying disabilities regardless of whether the student is eligible for services under the IDEA (2004). Closely tied to the tenets of Section 504, the Americans with Disabilities Act(2008) is a comprehensive, national mandate for the elimination of discrimination against individuals with disabilities and contains consistent, enforceable standards for addressing disability discrimination. Section 504 and the ADA are often cited together in cases that involve disability-based harassment claims in the context of public schools because the tests and remedies under each statute are the same. As the Second Circuit Court of Appeals observed in *Weixel v. Board of Education of N.Y.* (2002), other than Section 504's "limitation to denials of benefits 'solely' by reason of disability and its reach of only federally funded—as opposed to 'public'—entities, the reach and requirements of both statutes [Section 504 and the ADA] are precisely the same" (footnote 6).

A federal district court in *D.A. v. Meridian Joint School District No. 2* (2013) acknowledged that "school district liability for peer-on-peer disability-based harassment under Section 504 and the ADA has not been directly addressed by the United States Supreme Court" (at 628). Nevertheless, lower courts have entertained two potential theories of liability for disability-based bullying claims brought pursuant to Section 504 and the ADA: a *Davis* style deliberate indifference standard similar to that used in Title IX cases (with the added component of proving one's disability), and a *bad faith* or *gross misjudgment* standard. Kimmel and Alvarez (2013) describe the Davis-type deliberate indifference standard as a theory that is typically applied when a school district fails to adequately address bullying; and the *bad faith* or *gross misjudgment* standard may be applicable in situations where a school district fails to address bullying by making reasonable accommodations for students with disabilities.

A number of cases from the Fifth and Sixth Circuits demonstrate how the courts have addressed these claims. In *S.S. v. Eastern Kentucky University* (2008), the Sixth Circuit Court of Appeals used the following five-part test to analyze the plaintiff's disability-based peer-on-peer harassment claims under Section 504 and the ADA:

> (1) the plaintiff is an individual with a disability, (2) he or she was harassed based on that disability, (3) the harassment was sufficiently severe or pervasive that it altered the condition of his or her education and created an abusive educational environment, (4) the defendant knew about the harassment, and (5) the defendant was deliberately indifferent to the harassment. (at 454)

In this particular case, both parties agreed that the *Davis* standard as modified was the appropriate standard to be applied. The only question at issue was whether the defendant had been deliberately indifferent to the plaintiff's ongoing harassment. In finding that the plaintiff failed to prove the defendant was deliberately indifferent to ongoing disability-based harassment, the court noted the defendant's effort to investigate each matter reported to it, the other students were disciplined, and that each instance of harassment involved different circumstances, which did not establish a pattern. Further, the court found that the student instigated some of the problems and the school actively monitored the bullied students (S.S., 2008). This case demonstrates how difficult it is for a plaintiff to be successful bringing a disability-based discrimination case based on peer harassment using the *Davis* standard.

By comparison, the Fifth Circuit Court of Appeals in *Stewart v. Waco Independent School District* (2013) applied both the *Davis* standard and the *gross misjudgment* standard to the plaintiff's 504/ADA discrimination claims based on peer harassment. In *Stewart*, the plaintiff was a special-education student at the defendant's high school. After an incident involving sexual contact with another student, the plaintiff's Individualized Education Program (IEP) was modified to require close supervision and separation from male students. Nevertheless, the plaintiff was involved in three additional incidents of sexual conduct over the next 2 years, which prompted her lawsuit under Section 504 and the ADA. The court found the plaintiff's pleadings to be insufficient to support a claim that the defendant was deliberately indifferent to the plaintiff's disability-based harassment; however, the court did sustain her *gross misjudgment* claim. The court explained that alleging *gross misjudgment* is just another way of alleging that the defendant refused to provide reasonable accommodations. Furthermore, the "refusal" does not have to be an explicit refusal; it is enough to prove "professionally unjustifiable conduct" (Stewart, 2013, at 523). In allowing the plaintiff's *gross*

Asserting Multiple Claims to Establish School District Liability

In *Sutherlin v. Independent School District No. 40 of Nowata County, Oklahoma* (2013), the plaintiffs brought multiple claims against their son's school district based on a record of constant bullying over a long period of time, which left their son depressed and withdrawn. The plaintiffs' son qualified for special-education programs and services under IDEA as a student with a learning disability. According to the plaintiffs, the school district not only failed to address the peer harassment and enforce its own zero-tolerance policies, but engaged in bullying behavior of its own. The *Sutherlin* case presents a smorgasbord of claims brought against the defendants, including Section 1983 claims for violating the Due Process Clause and the Equal Protection Clause of the Fourteenth Amendment, claims pursuant to Section 504 and the ADA, as well as a breach of contract claim rooted in state law based on the district's failure to enforce its own policies and a negligence claim based on state tort law.

While numerous claims were asserted in *Sutherlin* (2013), only a couple survived the defendant's motion for summary judgment. The court dismissed the plaintiffs' claim that the defendant violated the substantive due process rights of their son by failing to protect him from peer harassment. In order to prevail on such a claim, a plaintiff must show that the defendant's conduct (viewed in its entirety) was conduct that "shocks the conscience." This is an incredibly high standard to meet, and the court in *Sutherlin* found that even if the defendant exercised poor judgment or exhibited insensitivity, it was not enough to sustain a claim for violating the Due Process Clause of the Fourteenth Amendment. Not surprisingly, Kimmel and Alvarez (2013) observed that most substantive due process claims based on peer harassment are unsuccessful.

By contrast, the court in *Sutherlin* (2013) allowed the plaintiffs' Equal Protection claim to proceed to trial based on the court's finding that plaintiffs had produced enough evidence that a reasonable jury could conclude that their son was treated differently than others similarly situated. Likewise, the plaintiffs' Section 504 and ADA claims also survived based on the plaintiffs' allegations that the defendants were "deliberately indifferent" by failing to take any action that would cause the harassment to cease after the plaintiffs and others repeatedly reported the bullying incidents. Another of plaintiffs' claims was based on a breach of contract theory as the plaintiffs alleged the bullying policies in the Student Code of Conduct created an implied contract that the defendant failed to uphold. The court found that the parties lacked the "consideration" needed to establish an implied contract, in part because the plaintiffs' son was required to attend school and abide by its policies under the compulsory laws of the state of Oklahoma.

Finally, the court dismissed the plaintiffs' negligence claim as well on technical grounds related to deficient pleadings; however, the court did open the possibility for the plaintiffs to amend their original complaint as a way of rehabilitating the negligence claim.

Sutherlin (2013) is illustrative of the type of cases being filed in federal courts (with seemingly increased frequency) against school districts based on peer bullying. In fact, earlier cases such as *S.S. v. Eastern Kentucky University* (2008) also proceeded under multiple claims theories. The plaintiffs in *S.S.* asserted claims against a university-run laboratory school based on peer harassment that included Section 504 and ADA claims, Section 1983 claims for substantive and procedural due process violations as well as equal protection violations, and claims for negligence and intentional infliction of emotional distress rooted in state law. All claims were ultimately dismissed by the Sixth Circuit Court of Appeals. Plaintiffs are finding varying degrees of success establishing school district liability for student-on-student bullying based on legal theories that include the deprivation of constitutional rights, deprivation of civil rights, and even state claims rooted in the law of torts.

Although many of the bullying cases have primarily relied on federal claims, several of the recent cases also incorporated varying state claims theories. Further, with every state other than Montana (as of 2014) now having state bullying laws, it is important to be aware not only of the applicable federal statutes but also of the many state laws that may have direct liability implications for school districts and that may remove barriers to educational opportunities for students who are bullied. The rest of this chapter provides an analysis of the strengths and weaknesses of those laws (as well as the duties they impose on school districts) as measured by the U.S. Department of Education's guidelines for individuals charged with revising or creating effective bullying statutes (DOE, 2010).

ELEVEN KEY COMPONENTS IN STATE BULLYING LAWS

In a December 2010 Dear Colleague Letter, the U.S. Department of Health and Human Services and the U.S. Department of Education published guidelines considered key to the formation of effective bullying legislation (DOE, 2010). These guidelines, drawn from research and evidence-based practices, were designed to assist states in the creation of statutes that would identify definitional parameters of bullying, the location and conditions wherein school districts are responsible for acts of bullying, and encourage the development of the policy and procedures to protect both the victim and the bully. While the federal government strongly encourages states to use the bullying guidelines to create bullying statutes, there is no mandate to do so. To obtain a perspective on state bullying legislation, the bullying statutes of 49 states were analyzed for the inclusion of the federally suggested key elements. The analysis data is reported by the individual key elements.

Purpose Statement

The first component suggested by federal bullying guidelines is the Purpose Statement. In this component, schools are encouraged to describe the impact bullying has on students, including student learning, school safety, student engagement, and the school environment. The federal guidelines also suggest that the Purpose Statement discuss the reasons bullying is not acceptable and set the tone for administration, staff, students, parents, and community to take bullying seriously.

A review of state statutes shows that 42 states have incorporated a Purpose Statement into their bullying laws while eight state statutes do not have a Purpose Statement (see Appendix A). This data show that a high percentage of state statutes have chosen to outline the reasons why bullying is inappropriate and how bullying has a negative impact on both students and the learning environment.

As an example of state statutes setting the tone for the importance of negating bullying behavior, Oklahoma's bullying statute states that bullying negatively impacts schools and society as a whole and announces that bullying is not to be tolerated.

> The Legislature finds that bullying has a negative effect on the social environment of schools, creates a climate of fear among students, inhibits their ability to learn, and leads to other antisocial behavior. Bullying behavior has been linked to other forms of antisocial behavior, such as vandalism, shoplifting, skipping and dropping out of school, fighting, and the use of drugs and alcohol. Successful programs that recognize, prevent, and effectively intervene in bullying behavior have been developed and replicated in schools across the country. These schools send the message that bullying behavior is not tolerated and, as a result, have improved safety and created a more inclusive learning environment. (School Safety and Bullying Prevention Act, 2009)

Statement of Scope

Per the federally suggested guidelines, a Statement of Scope should address the school's jurisdiction over places where bullying might occur. The guidelines recommend policies that identify specifics such as the campus, school-sponsored activities or events, school-provided transportation, and school-owned technology. One state does not have a Statement of Scope, while 48 state statutes do have a Statement of Scope (see Appendix A). From this data, it can be seen that a majority of the states have clearly established where and when a school district is responsible for responding to and overseeing bullying complaints.

Indiana statute provides an example of how a Statement of Scope might specify when the school district is responsible (and accountable) for addressing bullying issues.

> The discipline rules [related to bullying]... must apply when a student is: (1) on school grounds immediately before or during school hours, immediately after school hours, or at any other time when the school is being used by a school group; (2) off school grounds at a school activity, function, or event; (3) traveling to or from school or a school activity, function or event; or (4) using property or equipment provided by the school. (Discipline Rules Prohibiting Bullying Required, 2010)

Specification of Prohibited Conduct

The federal guidelines recommend the Specification of Prohibited Conduct section of a bullying statute should provide the specific characteristics of bullying and cyberbullying and should also include a nonexclusive list of specific bullying behaviors. In addition, for purposes of establishing a clear definition and expectations regarding bullying, the statute should state that bullying includes intentional efforts to harm one or more individuals, may be verbal or nonverbal, and is not limited to behaviors that result in physical harm. While 47 states have statements in their statutes that address prohibited conduct, 2 states fail to address the characteristics of bullying and cyberbullying (see Appendix A).

Although it is recommended that statutes include information on both bullying and cyberbullying, several states have statutes that include prohibited conduct on only one of the two components. For example, Florida's statute details the bullying characteristics.

> "Bullying" means systematically and chronically inflicting physical hurt or psychological distress on one or more students... (d) The definitions of "bullying" and "harassment" include: (1) Retaliation against a student or school employee by another student or school employee for asserting or alleging an act of bullying or harassment... [and] (2) Perpetuation of [bullying or harassing] conduct... by an individual or group with intent to demean, dehumanize, embarrass, or cause physical harm to a student. (Bullying and Harassment Prohibited, 2010)

Investigating and Responding to Bullying

The federal guidelines suggest LEAs adopt procedures for promptly investigating and responding to any report of bullying and that the school district be required to notify all involved parties regarding procedures for contacting law enforcement should the need arise. A total of 35 states have procedures for investigating and responding to bullying but 14 states do not (see Appendix A).

For example, Massachusetts state law states that the school principal must investigate reported cases of bullying, contact law enforcement if a criminal act has been committed, and notify parents of both the victim and the bully (School Bullying Prohibited, 2013).

Written Records

The federal bullying guidelines recommend state statutes include language that encourages local education agencies (LEAs) to identify a process that creates and maintains detailed records, including the resolution, of all bullying incidents. Some 21 states have record maintenance requirements, 28 states do not (see Appendix A). A majority of states do not require LEAs to maintain records of the bullying incidents that occur in the district. Thus, with the lack of required recordkeeping, at any given time it is extremely difficult to collect accurate data on the number and severity of bullying instances. California state statute mandates that the state Department of Education is responsible for assessing whether local educational agencies are compliant with reporting and is also responsible for conducting annual reviews (Safe Place to Learn Act, 2011).

Sanctions

The federal bullying guidelines suggest that LEAs create detailed descriptions of a graduated range of consequences and sanctions for bullying. A total of 45 states have consequences and sanctions in place and 4 states do not specify disciplinary sanctions (see Appendix A). However, it should be noted that while 91.8% of the state statutes require consequences and sanction, the statutes did not require the itemization or creation of tiered or laddered levels of discipline. The four states whose bullying legislation does not contain discipline plans run the risk of not being prepared to appropriately discipline acts of bullying.

Referrals

The federal bullying guidelines suggest LEAs have procedures for referring victims, perpetrators, and others to counseling, mental health, and/or other health services as appropriate. Some 13 states have referral procedures in place, whereas 36 states do not (see Appendix A). Maryland's statutory referral process focuses on providing "support services to the student bully, to the victim, and any bystanders" (Model Policy Prohibiting Bullying, 2010).

Review of Local Policies

The federal bulling guidelines suggest that states review local policies on a regular basis to ensure the goals of the states' statutes are being met. Analysis shows that 42.9% of state bullying statutes address the issue of policy renewal, which means that 57.1% of states have not set a timeframe to revisit their bullying statutes (see Appendix A). As an example, Illinois' statute establishes a 2-year expectation for LEAs to review and update local policies and places the responsibility for monitoring bullying policies on the Illinois State Board of Education (Bullying Prevention, 2013).

Communication Plan

The federal guidelines for bullying policy recommend that communication plans be in place to notify students, families, and staff of policies related to bullying, including the consequences for engaging in bullying or be ing a bystander who takes no action. A total of 44 states have requirements for communication plans and 5 states do not (see Appendix A). According to Arkansas state law, communication plans are required to identify the behaviors that constitute bullying, that bullying is prohibited, and the consequences for bullying. The Arkansas statute also requires the communication plan be "conspicuously posted in every classroom, cafeteria, restroom, gymnasium, auditorium, and school bus in the district, [and the] notices must be provided to parents, students, school volunteers, and employees" (Antibullying Policies, 2007).

Training and Preventive Education

The federal bullying guidelines recommend proper training in the areas of prevention, identification, and response to bullying for all school district employees. The guidelines also recommend school districts implement age-appropriate bullying prevention programs for students. Data shows that 41 states have policies that require training for bullying while 8 states do not require bullying training for staff or students (see Appendix A).

South Carolina's law is an example of a statute that requires local districts to incorporate information regarding harassment, intimidation, or bullying into a training program for school employees and volunteers who have significant contact with students (Local School Districts to Adopt Policies Prohibiting Harassment, 2009). Additionally school staff, students, administrators, volunteers, parents, law enforcement, and community members are encouraged to be involved in the establishment of bullying prevention programs and other initiatives (Local School Districts to Adopt Policies Prohibiting Harassment, 2009).

Transparency and Monitoring

The federal bullying guidelines suggest LEAs annually report the number of bullying incidents and the schools' responses to the state. Currently, 21 state statutes include transparency and monitoring language while 28 do not have the language (see Appendix A). These statistics are consistent with the subcomponent of Written Reports, where 57.1% of states do not require LEAs to generate written documentation of bullying incidents; and the data for this Transparency and Monitoring component indicates that the same percentage of state policies (57.1%) do not require LEAs to submit reports to the state. New York's statute is an example that addresses the transparency and monitoring component through an annual reporting mandate of incidents (Discrimination and Harassment Prohibited, (2010).

Statement of Rights to Other Legal Recourse

Per the federal bullying guidelines, LEAs should have a policy statement which does not preclude bullying victims from seeking legal remedies outside the LEA's discipline plan. Some 21 states have statutes with statements pertinent to seeking legal remedy, and 28 states do not have statutes that address additional legal remedy (see Appendix A).

As an example, Oregon's statement of rights to other legal recourses states, "[This statute] may not be interpreted to prevent a victim of harassment, intimidation or bullying or a victim of cyberbullying from seeking redress under any other available law, whether civil or criminal" (Victims May Seek Redress, 2009).

KEY COMPONENT SUMMARY

A ranking of state statutes based on the inclusion of the federal government's key components shows three states (Maryland, Maine, and New Jersey) have bullying statutes that contain all 16 key components; three states (Florida, New York, and Washington) have bullying statutes that contain 15 of the 16 criteria, and five states have bullying statutes that meet 14 of the 16 criteria (Alabama, Arkansas, New Hampshire, Oregon, and West Virginia). Since the key elements were drawn from research and evidence-based practices (DOE, 2010), it is likely the 11 state bullying statutes that include 90% or more of the recommended key elements have sound bullying policy. However, the ranking chart also shows that 13 state statutes contain fewer than 50% of the recommended elements (see Appendix B). The number of state statutes that address fewer than 50% of the recommended elements suggests multiple states may not have a clear definition of bullying nor do the statutes identify an understanding of processes and protections available for the bully, the victim, and the educational community.

The review of bullying statutes also revealed that the two most prevalent key elements are the Statement of Scope (addresses the locations and activities where a school has jurisdiction; 98.0%) and Development and Implementation of LEA Policies (policies developed collaboratively; 98.3%) (see Appendix A). The high percentage of states that have chosen to work collaboratively with various groups of state stakeholders to specify the location and types of activities where the school has jurisdiction (and responsibility) is a strong indicator that a majority of states are taking bullying seriously and are attempting to create policy that will help school districts reduce bullying on school property and at school functions (see Appendix A).

On the other end of the spectrum, the statute analysis indicates that 73.5 % of state statutes do not contain language requiring school districts to establish procedures for referring victims and bullies for services. The failure of state statutes to include the key component (Referral) could be an indicator that the state legislators see bullying as a behavior to be disciplined rather than remediated (see Appendix A).

To assist in the development of sound bullying state statutes and school district policies, this portion of the chapter briefly discussed each of the federally suggested key components and provided examples of state statutes that exemplify each of the key components. Additionally, appendices provide snapshots of the key elements and the number and percentage of states that have included the component in their bullying statutes (Appendix A), a ranking of states based on the number of key components found in statute (Appendix B), a listing of state laws pertinent to bullying (Appendix C), and a chart detailing the key components found in each state's bullying statutes (Appendix D).

CONCLUSION

At this time there are no federal laws that specifically address bullying (HHS, n.d.). However, in specific situations, students who are bullied may

APPENDIX A
Analysis of State Inclusion of Key Components in State Bullying Statute

		% of States	# of States
Purpose Statement	States That Have The Component	83.4%	41
	States That Do Not Have The Component	16.3%	8
Statement of Scope	States That Have The Component	98.0%	48
	States That Do Not Have The Component	2.0%	1
Specification of Prohibited Conduct	States That Have The Component	95.9%	47
	States That Do Not Have The Component	4.1%	2
Enumeration of Specific Characteristics	States That Have The Component	38.8%	19
	States That Do Not Have The Component	61.2%	30
Development and Implementation of LEA Policies	States That Have The Component	91.8%	45
	States That Do Not Have The Component	8.2%	4
Definition of Bullying	States That Have The Component	63.3%	31
	States That Do Not Have The Component	36.7%	18
Report Bullying	States That Have The Component	77.6%	38
	States That Do Not Have The Component	22.4%	11
Investigating and Responding to Bullying	States That Have The Component	71.4%	35
	States That Do Not Have The Component	28.6%	14
Written Reports	States That Have The Component	42.9%	21
	States That Do Not Have The Component	57.1%	28
Sanctions	States That Have The Component	91.8%	45
	States That Do Not Have The Component	8.2%	4
Referrals	States That Have The Component	26.5%	13
	States That Do Not Have The Component	73.5%	36
Review of Local Policies	States That Have The Component	42.9%	21
	States That Do Not Have The Component	57.1%	28
Communication Plan	States That Have The Component	89.8%	44
	States That Do Not Have The Component	10.2%	5
Training and Preventative Education	States That Have The Component	83.4%	41
	States That Do Not Have The Component	16.4%	8
Transparency and Monitoring	States That Have The Component	42.9%	21
	States That Do Not Have The Component	57.1%	28
Statement of Rights to Other Legal Recourse	States That Have The Component	42.9%	21
	States That Do Not Have The Component	57.1%	28

APPENDIX B
State Rank According to Inclusion of Suggested Federal Guidelines

State	Number of Components
Maryland	16
Maine	16
New Jersey	16
Florida	15
New York	15
Washington	15
Alabama	14
Arkansas	14
New Hampshire	14
Oregon	14
West Virginia	14
Delaware	13
Iowa	13
Massachusetts	13
North Carolina	13
North Dakota	13
Ohio	13
Vermont	13
California	12
Connecticut	12
Nevada	12
Wyoming	12
Louisiana	11
New Mexico	11
South Carolina	11
Tennessee	11
Virginia	11
Arizona	10
Illinois	10
Kentucky	10
Minnesota	10
Oklahoma	10
Georgia	9
Michigan	9
Pennsylvania	9
Rhode Island	9
Alaska	8
Colorado	8

(Continued)

APPENDIX B (continued)

State	Number of Components
Indiana	8
Mississippi	8
Utah	8
Wisconsin	8
Missouri	7
South Dakota	7
Hawaii	6
Texas	6
Idaho	5
Kansas	5
Nebraska	4

APPENDIX C
State Laws Pertinent to Bullying

Alabama

Alabama Code §16-28B-5—Student Harassment Prevention Act.

Alaska

Alaska Statute §14.33.200—Harassment, intimidation, and bullying policy.
Alaska Statute §14.33.210—Reporting of incidents of harassment, intimidation, or bullying.
Alaska Statute §14.33.200—Harassment, intimidation, and bullying policy.
Alaska Statute §14.33.210—Reporting of incidents of harassment, intimidation, or bullying.
Alaska Statute §14.33.220—Reporting; no reprisals.
Alaska Statute §14.33.230—Immunity from suit.
Alaska Statute §14.33.250—Definitions.

Arizona

Arizona Revised Statute §15-341.38—General powers and duties; immunity; delegation.

Arkansas

Arkansas Code Annotated §6-18-514(a) and (b)(1) and (2)—Anti-bullying policies.
Arkansas Code Annotated §6-18-514(b)(1)—Anti-bullying policies.
Arkansas Code Annotated §6-18-514(2)—Anti-bullying policies.

California
California Education Code §234.1- Safe Place to Learn Act
California Education Code §32261
California Education Code §32282

Colorado
Colorado Revised Statutes §22-32-109.1 (1) (b)—Board of Education—specific powers and duties -safe schools.

Connecticut
Connecticut General Statutes §10-145a—Teacher preparation-bullying training.
Connecticut General Statutes §10-220a—In-service training. Professional development committees.
Connecticut General Statutes §10-222d—Policy on bullying behavior.

Delaware
Delaware Code Annotated Title 14, §4112D—School bullying prevention.
Delaware Code Annotated Title 14, §4123A—School bullying prevention and criminal youth.

Florida
Florida Statutes Annotated §1006.147—Bullying and harassment prohibited.

Georgia
Georgia Code Annotated §20-2-751.4—Policies prohibiting bullying; assignment to alternative school; notice.

Hawaii
Hawaii State Board of Education Administrative Rule §8-19

Idaho
Idaho Code §18-917a—Student harassment, intimidation, bullying.

Illinois
105 Illinois Compiled Statutes §5/27=13.3 Internet Safety education Curriculum
105 Illinois Compiled Statutes §5/27-23.7—Bullying prevention.

Indiana
Indiana Code Annotated §20-33-8-0.2—Bullying.

North Dakota Century Code Chapter 15.1-19 -18—Bullying—Prohibition by Policy.

Ohio

Ohio Revised Code Annotated §3313.667—District bullying prevention initiatives.

Oklahoma

Oklahoma Statute Annotated Title 70, §24-100.2-5—School bullying prevention act.

Oregon

Oregon Revised Statute §339.351. Definitions

Oregon Revised Statute §339.353. Findings

Oregon Revised Statute §339.356. District policy required

Oregon Revised Statute §339.359. Training programs; prevention task forces, programs and other initiatives

Oregon Revised Statute §339.362. Retaliation against victims and witnesses prohibited; school employee immunity

Oregon Revised Statute §339.364. Victim may seek redress under other laws

Pennsylvania

Pennsylvania Consolidated Statute §1303.1-A—Policy relating to bullying.

Rhode Island

Rhode Island General Laws §16-21-34—Statewide bullying policy implemented.

South Carolina

South Carolina Code Annotated §59-63-140—Local school districts to adopt policies prohibiting harassment; required components; model policies by State Board of Education; bullying prevention programs.

South Dakota

South Dakota Codified Laws § 49-31-31—Harassing or Threatening Text Messages

Tennessee

Tennessee Code Annotated §49-6-4501- Legislative findings — Safety and civility.

Tennessee Code Annotated §49-6-4503. Development of policy regarding harassment, intimidation, bullying or cyber-bullying.

Tennessee Code §49-6-4504. Adoption of policy — Transmission of copy of policy to the commissioner of education.
Tennessee Code §49-6-4506. Task forces, programs or other initiatives.

Texas
Texas Education Code Annotated §25.0342—Transfer of students who are victims or have engaged in bullying.

Utah
Utah State Board of Education Policy §R227-613—School bullying and hazing policies and training.
Utah Code Annotated §53A-11a-102—Bullying and hazing definitions.
Utah Code Annotated §53A-11a-201– Bullying, cyber-bullying, harassment hazing, sexual battery and sexual exposure prohibited.
Utah Code Annotated §53A-11a-301–Bullying, cyber-bullying, harassment, hazing, and retaliation policy

Vermont
Vermont Statute Annotated Title 16, §570C–Bullying.

Virginia
Virginia Code Annotated §22.1-279.6—Board of education guidelines and model policies for codes of student conduct.

Washington
Washington Revised Code §28A.300.285—Harassment, intimidation, and bullying prevention policies and procedures.
Washington Revised Code §28A.300.2851—School Bullying and Harassment Work Group.
Washington Revised Code §28A.600.480—Reporting of harassment, intimidation, or bullying.

West Virginia
West Virginia Code Annotated §18-2C-3—Policy prohibiting harassment, intimidation or bullying .

Wisconsin
Wisconsin Statute §118.46—Policy on bullying.

Wyoming
Wyoming Statute Annotated §21-4-313—Prohibition against harassment, intimidation or bullying; reporting to school officials.

APPENDIX D: Rating Scale for State Bullying Laws

11 Key Components (0 = Not Contained in State Law; 1 = Contains Component in State Law)

State	Components of LEA Policies																
	Purpose	Statement of Scope	Prohibited Conduct	Enumeration of Specific a	LEA Policies	Definitions	Report Bullying	Investigating and Responding	Written Records	Sanctions	Referrals	Review of Local Policies	Communication Plan	Training and Preventive Education	Transparency and Monitoring	Statement of Rights to Other Legal Recourse	Total for State
AL	1	1	1	1	1	1	1	1	1	1	1	0	1	1	1	0	14
AK	1	1	1	0	1	0	1	0	0	1	0	0	1	0	1	0	8
AZ	1	1	0	0	1	1	1	1	1	1	1	0	1	0	0	0	10
AR	1	1	1	1	1	1	1	1	1	1	1	1	1	1	0	0	14
CA	0	1	1	1	1	0	1	1	1	1	0	1	1	1	1	0	12
CO	0	1	1	0	1	1	0	0	0	1	0	1	1	1	0	0	8
CT	0	1	1	0	1	0	1	1	1	1	1	1	1	1	1	0	12
DE	1	1	1	0	1	1	1	1	0	1	1	1	1	1	1	0	13
FL	1	1	1	1	1	1	1	1	1	1	1	1	1	1	1	0	15
GA	1	1	1	0	1	0	1	1	0	1	0	0	1	1	0	0	9
HI	1	1	1	1	0	0	0	0	0	0	0	0	0	0	1	1	6
ID	1	0	1	0	1	0	0	0	0	1	0	0	1	0	0	0	5
IL	1	1	1	1	1	0	0	0	0	1	0	1	1	1	0	1	10
IN	1	1	1	0	1	0	1	1	0	1	0	0	0	1	0	0	8
IA	1	1	1	1	1	1	1	1	0	1	0	0	1	1	1	1	13
KS	1	1	1	0	1	0	0	0	0	0	0	0	0	1	0	0	5
KY	1	1	1	0	1	0	1	1	0	1	0	0	1	1	1	0	10

(continued)

APPENDIX D: Rating Scale for State Bullying Laws (continued)

11 Key Components (0 = Not Contained in State Law; 1 = Contains Component in State Law)

State	Purpose	Statement of Scope	Prohibited Conduct	Enumeration of Specific a	LEA Policies	Definitions	Report Bullying	Investigating and Responding	Written Records	Sanctions	Referrals	Review of Local Policies	Communication Plan	Training and Preventive Education	Transparency and Monitoring	Statement of Rights to Other Legal Recourse	Total for State
	Components of LEA Policies																
LA	1	1	1	0	1	0	1	1	1	1	0	0	1	1	1	0	11
ME	1	1	1	1	1	1	1	1	1	1	1	1	1	1	1	1	16
MD	1	1	1	1	1	1	1	1	1	1	1	1	1	1	1	1	16
MA	1	1	1	0	1	1	1	1	0	1	1	1	1	1	0	1	13
MI	0	1	1	0	0	0	1	1	1	1	0	0	1	1	1	0	9
MN	0	1	1	1	1	1	1	1	0	1	0	0	1	1	0	0	10
MS	1	1	1	0	1	0	1	1	0	1	0	0	1	0	0	0	8
MO	0	1	1	0	1	0	1	0	0	1	0	0	1	1	0	0	7
NE	0	1	1	0	1	0	0	0	0	1	0	0	0	0	0	0	4
NV	1	1	1	0	1	1	1	0	1	1	0	1	1	1	1	0	12
NH	1	1	1	1	1	1	1	1	1	1	0	0	1	1	1	1	14
NJ	1	1	1	1	1	1	1	1	1	1	1	1	1	1	1	1	16
NM	1	1	1	1	1	1	1	1	0	1	0	0	1	1	0	0	11
NY	1	1	1	1	1	1	1	1	1	1	1	0	1	1	1	1	15
NC	1	1	1	1	1	1	1	1	0	1	0	1	1	1	0	1	13
ND	1	1	1	0	1	1	1	1	1	1	0	1	1	1	0	1	13
OH	1	1	1	0	1	1	1	1	1	1	0	0	1	1	1	1	13

(continued)

over 60% of LGBT students reported feeling unsafe due to their sexual orientation or gender expression (Kosciw et al., 2011, p. 19). While most students might report harassment and assault, the majority of LGBT students did not, mainly due to "doubts that staff would effectively address the situation or fears that reporting would make the situation worse in some way" (Kosciw et al., 2011, p. 27). Those who reported incidents characterized the response as somewhat ineffective (18.7%) or not at all effective (44.1%) (Kosciw et al., 2011, p. 37). Not surprisingly, high levels of victimization were associated with lower grade-point averages, higher truancy rates, depression, lack of a sense of belonging, and failure to pursue postsecondary education (Kosciw et al., 2011, p. 39). Teachers, principals, educational policymakers and legislators, by failing to satisfactorily address these issues, have been barriers to educational opportunities for LGBT youth. Similar levels of homophobia and transphobia were noted in Canadian schools in *The First National Climate Survey on Homophobia, Biphobia, and Transphobia in Canadian Schools* (Equality for Gays and Lesbians Everywhere [EGALE], 2011).

While there is much reason for concern, we also see reason for optimism. The findings of the GLSEN survey indicate that supportive staff, positive curricular representations, gay-straight alliances (GSAs), school-based antibullying/harassment policies, and comprehensive laws can result in safer and more positive environments (Kosciw et al., 2011, p. 57). Analysis of the climate survey results also indicates that LGBT students from states with comprehensive antibullying/harassment laws reported less hostile school climates, more positive resources, and more effective staff interventions. Developing positive school climates for LGBT students is complex and difficult work, which involves peer culture (Milner, 2004), educators' beliefs (Schneider & Dimito, 2008), and the wider social and political culture (Szalacha, 2003). As the American Educational Research Association Task Force on the Prevention of Bullying in Schools, Colleges and Universities (2013) writes, "Understanding the impact and implementation of law and the role of and relevance of a supportive legal context is fundamental to addressing bullying and harassment and making changes where necessary" (pp. 33–34).

The purpose of this study is to consider the impact of inclusive laws and school policies in Ontario, Canada, on the situation of LGBT youth in schools. Our thesis is that top-down equity and antibullying/harassment legislation and policy can contribute significantly to the development of school cultures that respect equity, engage students, and enhance learning. We begin with a summary of the legal context in Canada and the educational policy context in Ontario. The results of a survey of gay-straight advisors in Ontario are examined in order to consider the impact of the inclusive laws and policies on the activities of gay-straight alliances (GSAs) and on the response of educators to harassment and bullying (Kitchen & Bellini, 2013).

The Canadian Legal Context

While Canada is often perceived to be progressive in its laws and policies on sexual orientation, the emergence of LGBT rights is a relatively recent phenomenon in the country. In 1967, Pierre Trudeau, then Minister of Justice, presented *Bill C-150* decriminalizing same-sex activity. While his argument that "there is no place for the state in the bedrooms of the nation" (CBC, 1967) signaled a significant shift in the attitude of Canadians toward LGBT people, progress toward civil equality since then has been a long and incremental process. For example, Section 15 of the Canadian Charter of Rights and Freedoms did not grant human rights protection based on sexual orientation. It was not until 1995, in the case of *Egan v. Canada,* that the Supreme Court unanimously held that discrimination based on sexual orientation was unconstitutional. Today, all provinces in Canada have some version of a human rights code or act that protects gay rights. Same-sex marriage was recognized in 2003 and was legalized across Canada with the enactment of the Civil Marriage Act in 2005.

Two cases have proved significant in the move toward increased rights for LGBT students in Canada. In *Jubran v. North Vancouver School District No. 44,* Azmi Jubran claimed that he was repeatedly taunted, assaulted, kicked, spit on, and called a "faggot" and "homosexual" from 1993 to 1998. He filed a complaint with the British Columbia Human Rights Tribunal in 1996 arguing that his school had failed to protect him despite 12 documented incidents of harassment in a single year. School administrators admitted during court proceedings that sexual orientation was not specifically protected in the school's Code of Conduct and conceded that their progressive discipline approach had been unsuccessful in protecting Jubran. As they did nothing further to make Jubran safe from bullying, the board was deemed negligent and Jubran was awarded $4,500 in damages. In its ruling, the tribunal wrote, "There was evidence that resources were available to the school board to assist in dealing with homophobia and heterosexism in educational settings since at least 1992." On appeal, however, the board successfully argued that, since Jubran was heterosexual, the incidents did not involve sexual harassment. Jubran's 12-year ordeal ended when the B.C. Court of Appeal upheld the original decision. The significance of this case was twofold. First, it established that school boards had a legal obligation to address homophobia, and second, it indicated that homophobic language was unacceptable regardless of the sexual orientation of its target.

In *Hall (Litigation guardian of) v. Power* (2002), Justice McKinnon granted Marc Hall's request for an interlocutory injunction restraining Durham Catholic High School in Ontario from preventing him from attending the school dance with a male partner. While McKinnon affirmed the religious rights of Catholic schools in the area of curriculum, which is enshrined in the Constitution Act, 1867, his application of a general definition of the role of school under the Education Act led him to conclude that school dances were "not part of the religious education component of the Board's activity" and that the "restriction on Mr. Hall's activities is not proportionate." This interpretation of the curriculum meant that there was no reasonable basis for denying Hall access to "a fundamental [social] institution in the lives of young people." In effect, McKinnon had found "a way to allow an application that is in direct contrast to Catholic doctrine" (Oliverio & Manley-Casimir, 2009).

Both Jubran and Hall's cases illustrate systemic heterosexism and homophobia and the impact they have on students in Canadian schools. In *Jubran,* the school board denied its obligation to do more in response to homophobic bullying, even resorting to focusing on the fact that Jubran was heterosexual. In Hall's case, the Catholic school board treated this as an isolated incident, as if Hall were the only LGBT student in their schools. Grace and Wells refer to this as, "the pedagogy of negation that is meant to demean, dismiss, or fail to protect LGBTQ youth" (2005, p. 4). Both young men gained public attention as activists for greater rights under the Charter and human rights codes. Both cases alerted educators and school boards to the importance of respecting the human rights of all students, as the decisions suggest that the courts may be inclined to protect the rights of LGBT students in future cases. They also took place at a time when same-sex marriage became law without the political backlash that met American marriage equality efforts (Rayside, 2008).

The Educational Policy Landscape in Ontario

While LGBT students have often been the focus of debate and legislative efforts in the United States (Griffin & Oullett, 2003), they had largely been absent from education debates and legislation in Ontario until 2009 (Bellini, 2012). Under the leadership of Liberal Premier Dalton McGuinty and Minister of Education, Kathleen Wynne (2006–2010), equity issues that languished under the previous Progressive Conservative government were made priorities. Wynne established the Safe Schools Action Team (2008), which prepared a report titled *Shaping a Culture of Respect in our Schools: Promoting Safe and Healthy Relationship.* In investigating the complexities of safety in schools, the Team listened to gay and lesbian students who did not feel safe, comfortable, or respected by school staff. The report was highly critical of school boards' neglect of LGBT issues and revealed that educators were poorly trained in keeping LGBT students safe.

While the Team acknowledged that the issue of safety was multifaceted and that other minority students needed protection within the educational system, it did not shy away from naming homophobic harassment as a persistent problem that needed to be addressed immediately. The report recommended that safe schools training, including training addressing the prevention of homophobia, be provided by boards of education, the Ontario College of Teachers, faculties of education, principals' associations, and school boards. In response to this report, the Ontario Ministry of Education (OME) (2009b) amended the *Education Act* to address gender-based violence issues such as homophobia, sexual harassment, and inappropriate sexual behavior. *Realizing the Promise of Diversity: Ontario's Equity and Inclusive Education Strategy* (OME, 2009a) discussed the importance of creating a safe schools action team, antibullying groups, or a gay-straight alliance.

In response to the research and recommendations of the Safe Schools Action Team, two bills were passed two bills that amended the *Education Act.* Bill 212 (OME, 2007) introduced the words "bullying" and "homophobia" into legislation and, for the first time, LGBT students were named as a group entitled to protection and support. At the same time the Safe Schools Action Team was recommending amendments to the Eduction Act, lawyer Julian Falconer was hired by the Toronto District School Board to investigate school safety in Toronto secondary schools. *The Road to Health: A Final Report on School Safety* (Falconer, 2008) revealed that teachers and administrators who witnessed homophobia, gender-based violence, and bullying failed to keep students safe, and the report reinforced the message that teachers and administrators needed to be held accountable. This report, along with the Schools Action Team recommendations, led to a provision in Bill 157 (OME, 2009b), requiring educators and administrators to respond, report, and record in a timely manner all incidents of violence, including gender-based and homophobic violence. A disciplinary tribunal of the Ontario College of Teachers (2011), in *Tallevi v. the Ontario College of Teachers,* reinforced the importance of responding appropriately when it reprimanded an administrator for failure to report a serious incident of sexual abuse to the proper authorities.

The government of Ontario's commitment to fighting bullying and homophobia was further reinforced with the passage of *Bill 13: Accepting Schools Act* (OME, 2012a). It amended the *Education Act* to include a comprehensive process for school boards, administrators, and edutcators to follow in order to stop bullying. This involved educating all stakeholders—including

For the qualitative data analysis, we applied grounded theory (Strauss & Corbin, 1990), a methodology that allowed us to gather data "and then systematically develop theory directly derived from the data" (Walker & Myrick, 2006, p. 548). Anecdotal responses provided in the comment boxes were then analyzed through coding and categorizing of key idea units, as described by Creswell (2009). The idea units were collapsed into categorical clusters and themes representing participants' perceptions, then key overall findings and broad themes were identified. A more detailed explanation of the methodology, along with the complete survey results, is published elsewhere (Kitchen & Bellini, 2013).

For purposes of this chapter, we selectively draw on the findings of the larger study to highlight ways in which law and policy impact practices of inclusion and safety within schools. The first section focuses on the impact of GSAs, now enshrined in provincial legislation, on school climate. The next section focuses on the responses of educators—administrators and teachers—to harassment and bullying.

The Impact of Gay-Straight Alliances on School Climate

In Ontario, all public schools are mandated to permit gay-straight alliances if requested by students. Prior to this legislative change, many schools already had GSAs and many school districts already promoted GSAs as critical elements their equity and school climate strategies. In response to an open-ended question, 35 respondents (85.4%) reported that the presence of GSAs had a positive impact on school climate for LGBT-identified students, with three respondents uncertain and three not seeing effects up to that time. Well over half of the positive respondents were emphatic in their conviction that GSAs made a considerable difference. Among the anecdotal comments made by survey respondents were

- All students realize that there is support for the LGBT community in our school.
- Students feel that the presence of the GSA provides a "normalizing" effect on the school community.
- Yes, we have had assemblies, days of silence, and other events that inform the school of LGBT issues.
- Yes, we have reports from ex-students that it has helped and that, even if the students did not come, they felt that it was important to know that it was there.
- We have a strong GSA that monitors school safety for all LGBT students in our school.

- There has been a lot of emphasis on teaching through activities and our bulletin board. All students realize that there is support for the LGBTQ community in our school. Through the acquisition of knowledge comes comfort and understanding.

The efforts of GSAs, including monitoring by GSA advisors and members, seem to have helped increase accountability with administrators and teachers. GSA members and advisors often served as leaders in these efforts. As one participant noted, climate improved considerably "because of the presence of antibullying and the GSA initiatives." Other participants noted the role of GSA advisors as "vocal advocates" and noted the "normalizing effect [the GSA had] on the school community."

The Importance of GSAs in School Safety

Our findings, along with similar American data (e.g., Lipkin, 1999), dispel the common myth that GSAs are merely coming-out or counseling groups. Most of the activities of gay-straight alliances center on political action and awareness as well as social events. As such, they are a positive force for bottom-up reform by students and educators. Among those who recognize the positive impact of GSAs for LGBT students is the American Civil Liberties Union, which argues that GSAs make schools safer. "Research has shown that LGBT students hear fewer homophobic slurs, experience less harassment, have better attendance, and feel safer at schools that have GSAs" (ACLU, 2013). On January 25, 2012, the U.S. Department of Education declared the first-ever National Gay Straight Alliance Day.

> Bullying is an epidemic that has gone ignored for too long, and far too many of our young people are targeted and harassed based on their actual or perceived sexual orientation, gender identity, or gender expression. But across the country, Gay-Straight Alliances and other similar student groups are taking important steps to address these issues. (DOE, 2012)

The Ontario Ministry of Education, drawing on similar evidence, identified GSAs as a force of change in both its equity and inclusion policies and safe schools legislation. *Realizing the Promise of Diversity: Ontario's Equity and Inclusive Education Strategy* (2009a) and Progressive Discipline and Promoting Positive Student Behaviour (2012) address the need for a systemwide approach for school safety by fostering gay-straight alliances for example.

The Response of Educators to Harassment and Bullying

A major purpose of our survey was to identify the degree of homophobic harassment and bullying in Ontario schools. We asked participants to rate the overall climate, teasing and harassment, and the amount of bullying in their schools. Over 78% of respondents rated the overall climate as generally positive (5–7 rating), while over 56% rated their schools as safe for LGBT students. On the other side, while only 9.7% perceived schools to be unsafe overall (1–3 rating), 37.6% viewed schools as unsafe for LGBT youth. GSA advisors were evenly divided between those who rated the amount of teasing and verbal harassment of students as generally high (46.4%) and generally low (47.5%); most (73.2%) viewed it as moderately safe, neutral, or moderately unsafe (3–5 rating). More respondents (46.3%) rated bullying overall as low (1–3), with fewer (36.6%) identifying homophobic bullying as high and a large number regarding it as neutral (17.1%). On the other hand, homophobic bullying was rated as higher (42.5%) and lower (52.5%), with only 5% using the neutral rating. School size was a statistically significant factor, with the degree of bullying greatest in schools with fewer than 500 students and least in schools with more than 1,200 students.

As support by educators has been identified with positive results for LGBT students (EGALE, 2011; Kosciw et al., 2011), we were interested in the perceptions GSA advisors had regarding the efforts of their colleagues. We asked participants to rate the responses of teachers and administrators to teasing and verbal harassment and to bullying in their schools. After each, we asked them to rate these again in relation to homophobia/transphobia.

Teachers were generally viewed by the GSA advisors in the study as moderately effective in responding to teasing and verbal harassment, with 83.8% ranking them as between three and five on the seven-point scale. Interestingly, the response of teachers to homophobic harassment specifically was better, with 57.5% deemed to have addressed it effectively (5–7 rating). Advisors feel that more needs to be done to develop positive understandings and intervention strategies among teachers, rather than just reporting and punishing inappropriate student conduct.

The responses of administrators were viewed much more favorably. The responses of school administrators to teasing and verbal harassment were viewed as effective by 82.9% of respondents. Their response to homophobic harassment was viewed somewhat less favorably (78.1%), yet this too is significantly above the rating for teachers. Of particular note is the plurality ranked as highly effective (rating of 7) in their response to harassment generally (36.6%) and homophobic harassment (41.5%).

GSA advisors were also asked about provincial policies that might contribute to greater acceptance of minorities and improved school climate.

Some 98% were aware of the *Realizing the Promise of Diversity: Ontario's Equity and Inclusive Education Strategy* (OME, 2009a), with 56% rating implementation in their schools as positive (5–7 rating), while only 27% rated implementation as poor. While advisors commended administrators for their growing awareness of equity and bullying policies, as one participant noted, "We do still have to educate some teachers about the importance of using supportive and inclusive language at *all* times."

While there has been much progress, the results of our study suggest that LGBT teachers remain reluctant to disclose their identities to their peers and in particular to be open to students about their own sexual orientation. As a result, many were reluctant to be associated with the GSAs in their schools. Rather than blame these teachers, for whom the environment still appears unsafe, it is important that principals and school district officials find ways to make explicit their encouragement and support.

The Importance of Effective School Leadership for the Safety of LGBT Students

Recognition and protection of LGBT rights is the result of both activism at the grassroots level and incremental political and policy reforms. The American experience suggests that grassroots efforts that lack the support of administrators or policymakers have a limited institutional impact (Lipkin, 1999), while legislation and policy that lack support from educators and the community does little to change school climate (Szalacha, 2003).

Administrators face the daunting task of being management experts, visionaries, curriculum leaders, policy implementers, and much more (Stanford Educational Leadership Institute, 2005). When faced with multiple and competing demands, administrators and principals tend to give prior ity to the priorities identified by senior leadership and key stakeholders. As school safety is generally regarded as a top priority and one that administrators can influence, most strive to demonstrate their effectiveness on this measure.

All schools in Ontario must complete a *School Climate Survey* every 2 years, which includes staff, students, and parents. The results are submitted directly to the Ontario Ministry of Education, who review how effective policy and leadership has been in making schools more safe and accepting (OME, 2012a). School boards examine any discrepancies that may exist between principals' actions to keep the school safe (such as suspension rates) and student comments about the actual safety they experience. The board then makes recomendations to administrators on how to be more effective in addressing school safety.

ACKNOWLEDGEMENTS

This research is supported by a Dean's Research Initiative grant from the Dean of Education, Brock University.

REFERENCES

American Civil Liberties Union (ACLU). (2013, June 14). *How to start a gay straight alliance.* Retrieved July 5, 2013, from http://www.aclu.org/lgbt-rights/how-start-gay-straight-alliance-gsa

American Educational Research Association Task Force on the Prevention of Bullying in Schools, Colleges and Universities (2013). *Prevention of bullying in schools, colleges and universities: Research report and recommendations.* Washington, DC: American Educational Research Association.

Bellini, C. (2012). The pink lesson plan: Addressing the emotional needs of gay and lesbian students in teacher education. *Journal of LGBT Youth, 9*(4), 373–396. doi:10.1080/19361653.2012.714178

Canadian Broadcasting Corporation (CBC). (1967). Interview with Pierre Elliot Trudeau. *CBC Digital Archives.* Retrieved on May 22, 2015 from http://www.cbc.ca/player/Digital+Archives/Politics/Rights+and+Freedoms/Trudeau%27s+Omnibus+Bill+of+1969/ID/1815590962/

Canadian Charter of Rights and Freedoms (1982). Retrieved on May 22, 2015 from http://laws-lois.justice.gc.ca/eng/const/page-15.html.

Civil Marriage Act S.C. (2005), c. 33. Retrieved on May 22, 2015 from http://laws-lois.justice.gc.ca/eng/acts/c-31.5/page-1.html.

Constitution Act (1867). Retrieved on May 22, 2015 from http://laws-lois.justice.gc.ca/eng/const/page-1.html.

Creswell, J. W. (2009). *Research design: Qualitative, quantitative, and mixed method approaches* (3rd ed.). Thousand Oaks, CA: Sage.

Education Act R.S.O. (1990), c. E. 2. Retrieved on May 22, 2015 from http://www.ontario.ca/laws/statute/90e02

Elementary Teachers Federation of Ontario (ETFO) (2013). *Equity Workshops.* Retrieved on May 22, 2015 from http://www.etfo.ca/AboutETFO/Provincial-Office/EquityandWomensServices/Documents/Equity%20Workshops%202013-2014.pdf.

Equality for Gays and Lesbians Everywhere (EGALE) (2011). *Every class in every school: The final report on the first national climate survey on homophobia, biphobia, and transphobia in Canadian schools.* Retrieved June 2, 2013, from http://egale.ca/wp-content/uploads/2011/05/EgaleFinalReport-web.pdf

Egan v. Canada (1995) 2 S.C.R. 513. Retrieved on May 22, 2015 from http://scc-csc.lexum.com/scc-csc/scc-csc/en/item/1265/index.do.

Falconer, J. (2008). *The road to health: The final report on school safety.* Retrieved January 25, 2015, from http://www.falconerschoolsafetyreport.com/finalReport.html

Fink, A. (2013). *How to conduct surveys: A step-by-step guide.* Los Angeles, CA: Sage.

Grace, A. P., & Wells, K. (2005). The Marc Hall prom predicament: Queer individual rights v. institutional church rights in Canadian public education. *Canadian Journal of Education, 28*(3), 237–270.

Griffin, P., & Ouellett, M. (2003). From silence to safety and beyond: Historical trends in addressing lesbian, gay, bisexual, transgender issues in K–12 schools. *Equity & Excellence in Education, 36,* 106–114. doi:10.1080/10665680303508.

Hall (Litigation Guardian of) v. Powers, (2002) 213 D.L.R. (4th) 308 (Ont Sup Ct).

Houston, A. (2011, August 29). Toronto Catholic board to debate whether religion trumps rights of gay students. *DailyXtra.* Retrieved January 25, 2015, from http://www.xtra.ca/public/Toronto/Toronto_Catholic_board_to_debate_whether_religion_trumps_rights_of_gay_students-10685.aspx

Houston, A. (2012, June 4). Update: Ontario passes anti-bullying bill. *DailyXtra.* Retrieved June 1, 2013, from http://www.xtra.ca/public/National/UPDATE_Ontario_passes_antibullying_bill-12095.aspx

Houston, A. (2013, May 24). Toronto Catholic school board rejects GSA ban. *DailyXtra.* Retrieved January 25, 2015, from http://www.xtra.ca/public/National/Toronto_Catholic_school_board_rejects_GSA_ban-13618.aspx

Jubran v. North Vancouver School District No. 44, [2005] B.C.J. No. 733 (B.C.C.A.).

Kitchen, J., & Bellini, C. (2012). Addressing lesbian, gay, bisexual, transgender and queer (LGBTQ) issues in teacher education: Teacher candidates' perspectives. *Alberta Journal of Educational Research, 58*(3), 444–460.

Kitchen, J., & Bellini, C. (2013). Making schools safe and inclusive: Gay-straight alliances and school climate in Ontario. *Canadian Journal of Educational Administration and Policy, 146,* 1–37.

Kosciw, J. G., Diaz, E. M., Greytak, E. A., & Bartkiewicz, M. S. (2009). The 2009 National School Climate Survey. *Gay Lesbian Straight Educators Network.* Retrieved January 25, 2015, from http://files.eric.ed.gov/fulltext/ED512338.pdf

Kosciw, J. G., Greytak, E. A., Bartkiewicz, M. S., Boesen, M. J., & Palmer, N. A. (2011). The 2011 National School Climate Survey. *Gay Lesbian Straight Educators Network.* Retrieved from http://www.glsen.org/sites/default/files/2011%20National%20School%20Climate%20Survey%20Full%20Report.pdf

Lipkin, A. (1999). *Understanding homosexuality, changing schools.* Boulder, CO: Westview.

Milner, M., Jr. (2004). *Freaks, geeks and cool kids: American teenagers, schools and the culture of consumption.* New York, NY: Routledge.

Oliverio, C., & Manley-Casimir, M. (2009). The courts and the school: The judicial construction of the school. In M. Manley-Casimir & K. Manley-Casimir (Eds.), *The courts, the charter and the schools.* Toronto, Ontario, Canada: University of Toronto Press.

Ontario College of Teachers. (2010, May). *Additional qualification consultation on teaching LGBTQ students report and recommendations.* Retrieved January 25, 2015, from http://www.oct.ca/~/media/PDF/Additional%20Qualification%20Consultation%20on%20Teaching%20LGBTQ/aq_consultation_e.ashx

Ontario College of Teachers. (2011). *Ontario College of Teachers v. Silvio Joseph Tallevi.* Retrieved January 25, 2015, from http://www.oct.ca/ShowDocument.sample?documentType=Decision&id=551&lang=E

Ontario Ministry of Education (OME). (2007). *Bill 212, Education Act Amendment* (Progressive Discipline and School Safety). S.O. 2007 C-14.

Ontario Ministry of Education (OME). (2009a). *Realizing the Promise of Diversity: Ontario's Equity and Inclusive Education Strategy.*

Ontario Ministry of Education (OME). (2009b). *Bill 157: Education Act Amendment* (Keeping Our Kids Safe at School). S.O. 2009, c. 17.

Ontario Ministry of Education (OME). (2012a). *Bill 13: Education Act Amendment* (Accepting Schools). S.O. 2009, c. 13.

Ontario Ministry of Education (OME). (2012b). *Education Act,* R.S.O. 1190, c.E.2, Section 13: Behaviour Discipline and Safety, Articles 303.1, 303.2, 303.3.

Ontario Ministry of Education (OME) (2012c). *Progressive Discipline and Promoting Positive Student Behavior: Policy/Program Memorandum.* No. 145. Retrieved on May 22, 2015 from https://www.edu.gov.on.ca/extra/eng/ppm/145.pdf.

Ontario Secondary School Teachers Federation (OSSTF). (2012). Educational services workshops. *OSSTF/FEESO.* Retrieved January 25, 2015 from, http://www.osstf.on.ca/edservicesworkshops

Rayside, D. (2008). *Queer inclusions, continental divisions: Public recognition of sexual diversity in Canada and the United States.* Toronto, Ontario, Canada: University of Toronto Press.

Rayside, D. (2010, June). *Sex ed in Ontario: Religious mobilization and socio-cultural anxiety.* Paper presented at the Annual Meeting of the Canadian Political Science Association. Concordia University, Montreal, Quebec, Canada.

Ryan, J. (2006). *Inclusive leadership.* San Francisco, CA: Jossey-Bass.

Safe Schools Action Team. (2008). *Shaping a culture of respect in our schools: Promoting safe and healthy relationships.* Toronto, Ontario, Canada: Ontario Ministry of Education.

Schneider, M., & Dimito, A. (2008). Educators' beliefs about raising lesbian, gay, bisexual, and transgender issues in schools: The experience in Ontario, Canada. *Journal of LGBT Youth, 5*(4), 49–71. doi:10.1080/19361650802223003

Stanford Educational Leadership Institute. (2005). *School leadership study: Developing successful principals.* Retrieved on May 22, 2015 from https://eshacommunity.wikispaces.com/file/view/School_Leadership_Study.pdf.

Strauss, A., & Corbin, J. (1990). *Basics of qualitative research: Grounded procedures and techniques.* Newbury Park, CA: Sage.

Szalacha, L. A. (2003). Safer sexual diversity climates: Lesson learned from an evaluation of Massachusetts safe schools program for gay and lesbian students. *American Journal of Education, 110*(1), 58–88. doi:10.1086/377673

U.S. Department of Education (DOE). (2012, January 25). A special message on national gay straight alliance day. *HomeRoom* [blog]. Retrieved July 5, 2013, from http://www.ed.gov/blog/2012/01/a-special-message-on-national-gay-straight-alliance-day/

Walker, D., & Myrick, F. (2006). Grounded theory: An exploration of process and procedure. *Qualitative Health Research, 16*(4), 547–559. doi:10.1177/1049732305285972

Withers, J. (2013, June 22). US Department of Education will start collecting anti-gay bullying data from across the country. *Gay Star News*. Retrieved January 25, 2015, from http://www.gaystarnews.com/article/us-department-education-will-start-collecting-anti-gay-bullying-data-across-country220613

CHAPTER 9

USE OF DISPOSITION CRITERIA IN THE APPROVAL PROCESS OF TEACHER CANDIDATES BY SCHOOLS OF EDUCATION

Lawrence T. Kajs, Bettye Grigsby, and Kent A. Divoll

INTRODUCTION

The community trusts that school districts provide qualified teachers to instruct their children in early childhood (EC) to 12th-grade classrooms. In turn, the school districts expect schools of education at colleges and universities to certify and graduate teachers who possess content knowledge, pedagogical foundations, and professional dispositions. In the teacher preparation process, schools of education are guided by the state education agency, state higher-education body, and regional higher-education accreditation association, for example, Southern Association of Colleges and Schools (SACS), in the conferral of degrees and certifications on teacher candidates.

A key element of the preparation process is ensuring graduates have dispositions (i.e., belief, attitudes, and values) expected by the teaching

Law and Education Inequality, pages 149–158

profession. National teacher accreditation organizations provide guidance and support regarding disposition criteria in the teacher certification process. If a teacher preparation program does not address its set disposition criteria, national accreditation standing could be jeopardized or even revoked. If the teacher preparation program decides to terminate a student's participation in pursuing teacher certification for not meeting set disposition criteria, the possibility of legal action by the dismissed student could occur. In fact, federal courts have heard several student-initated cases on this topic in the past few years (Oyama v. University Of Hawaii, 2013; Reichert v. Elizabethtown College, 2012; Winkle v. Ruggieri, 2013).

This chapter will discuss the relevant use of disposition criteria in the preparation process of teacher candidates: (a) a brief literature review on the use and assessment of disposition criteria (or teacher qualities) in teacher education programs; (b) court cases that address the use of disposition criteria in the approval/removal process of teacher candidates; and (c) recommended policies, regulations, and practices that can facilitate and support the application of disposition criteria in the approval process of teacher candidates in schools of education.

DISPOSITION CRITERIA IN TEACHER PREPARATION PROGRAMS

Teacher candidates need to acquire the necessary content knowledge and appropriate pedagogical skills to be instructors in EC to 12th-grade classrooms. Moreover, these students are expected to possess certain professional dispositions, such as responsibility and fairness in effectively addressing the educational needs of EC to 12th-grade students (Kent State University. 2013). Disposition criteria are typically defined by the national accreditation bodies for schools of education. The National Council for Accreditation of Teacher Education (NCATE), which has been a primary national accreditation body for education preparation providers, has defined professional dispositions as "Professional attitudes, values, and beliefs demonstrated through both verbal and non-verbal behaviors as educators interact with students, families, and colleagues, and communities" (NCATE, 2015). Individual higher-education institutions can adapt terminology and wording in listing and defining specific disposition criteria (NCATE, 2015).[1]

In July 2013, NCATE merged with another accreditation entity, the Teacher Education Accreditation Council (TEAC), to form the Council for the Accreditation of Educator Preparation (CAEP, 2013). The new CAEP standards have expanded the understanding of professional dispositions to suggest that teacher candidates and completers of teacher education programs must "nurture the academic and social development of all students through professional dispositions such as caring, fairness, and the belief that all students can learn."[2]

In teacher preparation programs, especially those holding national accreditation, administrators and faculty have the duty to the profession and the public to ensure that teacher candidates demonstrate satisfactorily set professional dispositions (University of Memphis, 2008). If the teacher preparation program does not have an assessment process in place for appropriate dispositions, national accreditation can be at risk or possibly rescinded.

The assessment of student behaviors, which include verbal and nonverbal interactions, typically uses "observable behaviors in educational settings" (CAEP, 2013). However, at times, professional dispositions can be difficult to clearly evaluate because of the abstract nature of some disposition criteria (e.g., fairness). Thus, evaluations of students are regularly conducted by administrators, faculty, and mentor-teachers throughout the matriculation period to ensure all established disposition criteria are being met at the acceptable level (Kent State University, 2013). For example, at the University of Memphis, educators (i.e., university instructors, supervisors for student teachers, or mentor teachers) working with teacher candidates can fill out a disposition form on a candidate at any time for 1 or more of the 16 dispositions on its evaluation form (University of Memphis, 2008). If a candidate's rating needs improvement on one or more disposition criteria, a remediation plan of action can be initiated along with periodic follow-up discussions with advisors until the process is completed (University of Memphis, 2008). If a student is judged as not meeting all disposition criteria, there are three possible options: (a) allowing the candidate to continue, (b) requiring the candidate to follow a remediation plan, or (c) recommending dismissal from the teacher certification program (University of Memphis, 2008).

In conducting the assessment of set disposition criteria, schools of education should institute clear and explicit policies and procedures (e.g., due process guidelines). Doing so can help to assist and protect students and to safeguard teacher education program faculty, administrators, and mentor-teachers, as well as the EC to 12th-grade school community where teacher candidates may potentially work (CAEP, 2013). However, even with clear and explicit regulations in place, the possibility of legal action by a dismissed teacher candidate can occur.

COURT CASES ON DISPOSITION CRITERIA IN TEACHER EDUCATION PROGRAMS

In the last few years, litigation has occurred in multiple U.S. District Courts where teacher education students have brought legal action against higher-education institutions and their faculty/administrators on the application

Winkle took legal action in the U.S. District Court Southern District of Ohio Eastern Division. As the plaintiff, proceeding *pro se* (i.e., on one's own behalf), Winkle requested a motion for a Temporary Restraining Order and a motion for a Preliminary Injunction. He brought these legal actions against Ohio University faculty and employees. As plaintiff, he alleged multiple violations including the First Amendment (right of free speech), Fourteenth Admendment (right to due process), and Equal Protection Clause (discrimination that was based on age/gender; reprisal for entering charges of race/gender discrimination).

The U.S. District Court Southern District of Ohio Eastern Division denied the plaintiff's motions, since evidence did not demonstrate the plaintiff was denied his fundamental rights. This case reiterated a key point regarding the professional judgment of higher-education faculty and employees. "Once again, the Court is reluctant to second-guess the judgment of academic professionals regarding the qualifications of teaching" (Winkle v. Ruggieri, 2013).

Oyama v. University of Hawaii (2013)

In the summer of 2010, Mark Oyama enrolled in the College of Education's Post Baccalaureate Certificate Teaching Program at the University of Hawaii. He wanted to complete the preparation process in secondary education so he could apply to the Hawaii Teacher Standards Board to obtain a teacher license. The program's handbook indicated that the mission of the College of Education was to prepare educators who are not only knowledgeable and effective professionals, but also caring. To this end, educators are expected to show a high level of professionalism by demonstrating the following disposition criteria: competence, ethical behavior, reflection, respect for diversity, fairness, as well as a commitment to inclusion and social responsibility. The handbook also noted that the conceptual framework of the college was aligned with standards of the following organizations: NCATE, National Education Association (NEA), and Hawaii Teacher Standards Board.

In the summer of 2010, one of Oyama's professors expressed concern to the Teaching Program Director about Oyama's viewpoints on the role and responsibilities as well as the characteristics of a school teacher. In the fall of 2010, another professor expressed concerns about Oyama's perspective on two topics—the age of consent and online child predators. This was troublesome to the professor since a teacher is responsible for the safety of students. The professor even spoke with Oyama about his viewpoints. The professor thought the teaching program should be careful about accepting Oyama as a teacher candidate because of his lack of sensitivity to and empathy with others as well as his lack of self-awareness. A third professor raised a concern about Oyama's unreasonable strategies in teaching students who have disabilities.

Moreover, the Field Experience Coordinator completed an assessment form regarding Omaya's teaching qualities. Omaya received an unacceptable rating in 7 of 15 areas. These seven areas included (a) application of sound judgment, (b) professionalism in appearance and mannerism, (c) collaboratively working with others, (d) enthusiasm in teaching and students, (e) effectiveness in teaching, (f) self-reflecting, and (g) acceptance of feedback and suggestions. However, Oyama was found acceptable regarding competency of subject matter.

At a meeting with the Director of Teaching, the University Coordinator for Field Experience, and an official from the Office of Student Academic Services, Omaya was told that his application for student teaching was denied based on his evaluations—he did not meet the national and state teaching standards. Omaya sent a letter to the Academic Grievance Committee and the Director of Teaching in which he appealed the decisions denying him the student teaching opportunity. The Director of Teaching denied his request for student teaching and his alternative request for a refund of tuition for all prior coursework he had finished in the College of Education. The director told him that he could submit an appeal to the Academic Grievance Committee. Omaya then sent an email to the Vice Chancellor of Academic Affairs requesting that his appeal be reviewed. The Office of Academic Affairs referred the appeal to the Dean of Education because of the Dean's knowledge of the college's programs and professional standards. The Dean formed a grievance committee to investigate Omaya's complaint/appeal. The grievance committee and Dean affirmed the earlier decision to deny Omaya a student teaching position.

The plaintiff, Omaya, took legal action in the U.S. District Court for the District of Hawaii. As plaintiff, he alleged multiple violations, including the First Amendment (right of free speech), Fourteenth Admendment (right to due process), and 42 U.S.C. § 1983 (deprivation of rights), as well as Article I, §§ 2, 4, 5, and 6 of the Hawaii State Constitution (rights of individuals; freedom of speech, press, religion, petition, as well as assembly; equal protection and due process; and right to privacy). The plaintiff sought both injunctive relief and damages; and for partial summary judgment with regard to the matter of liability. The U.S. District Court for the District of Hawaii denied/dismissed all the plaintiff's motions and claims since the plaintiff failed to show his constitutional rights were violated. In fact, the evidence demonstated that the defendants exercised their professional judgment in discerning whether or not teacher candidates embody the dispositions for being a qualified classroom teacher. The plaintiff's claims for monetary relief from the defendants was barred by the Eleventh Amendment (qualified immunity) since they acted in their official capacities. The court granted the defendants' motion for summary judgment. This case illustrated two key points with regard to higher educational institutions:

1. The First Amendment does not require Defendants to accept Plaintiff in a student teaching program if in their judgment he did not meet State and National teaching standards (Oyama v. University of Hawaii, 2013).
2. The United States Supreme Court has consistently exercised judicial deference to a University's academic dismissal decisions out of respect for the University's professional judgment (Oyama v. University of Hawaii, 2013).

RECOMMENDED POLICIES AND PROCEDURES IN ADDRESSING THE USE OF DISPOSITIONS

The courts have upheld the decisions of colleges and universities to apply disposition criteria in the assessment of students in teacher preparation programs. However, there could be future legal challenges from teacher candidates who have been dismissed from the preparation/certification program for not meeting mimimum standards on set disposition criteria. Thus, schools of education may want to implement the following recommended guidelines to formally advise faculty and education students about the use of dispositions which may help to lessen legal exposure to the higher-education institution:

1. Develop mission and goal statements that clearly address the value of professional dispositions in describing its teacher preparation program's modus operandi (i.e., how the organization operates), placing this information on the school of education website and possibly on course syllabi as well.
2. Develop and update a manual that clearly defines and describes disposition criteria as well as the criteria's purpose and benefits, and the process used to assess students' dispositions. This process can serve to guide teacher candidates, faculty, administrators, mentor-teachers, and staff in their duties and responsibilities. The placement of this information on the school of education website can provide convenient access to this information.
3. Recommend to school districts that they include in teacher employment postings the need for applicants to possess professional dispositions. Morover, the professional dispositions of applicants should be addressed in interview questions and reference checks.

4. Have education students, at the beginning of the program, sign and date an application form that includes language about the need to successfully address professional disposition criteria as required by the teacher education program.
5. Develop a mentoring program (and provide mentoring training to teacher supervisors) that supports teacher candidates in applying professional disposition criteria in the context of classroom teaching.
6. Establish a system of recordkeeping in documenting teacher candidates' actions in meeting an acceptable level on set professional disposition criteria. This ongoing documentation allows the organization to track performance and provide the requisite supervisory feedback and professional development that teacher candidates may need and provides opportunities for teacher candidates to self-assess their dispositions based on defined activities/experiences in the program.
7. Develop a review system to ensure due process (e.g., academic grievance committee) for teacher candidates who are dimissed from the teacher preparation program for not meeting the requisite level on set disposition criteria.

NOTES

1. For example, Kent State University's teacher education guidelines include verbiage where "teacher candidates are expected to demonstrate: (1) Fairness by striving to meet the educational needs of all students in a caring, non-discriminatory, and equitable manner; (2) Belief that all students can learn; (3) Responsibility; and (4) Professionalism." (Kent State University, 2015).
2. According to CAEP's 2013 annual report, 49% of all of the education preparation providers as of 2011 and 62% of candidates who are preparing to teach have CAEP accreditation. The merging of these organizations can provide opportunities for consistency in the use of disposition criteria in the teacher preparation process (CAEP, 2013).

SUMMARY

Professional dispositions have been found to be critical in supporting teacher effectiveness in the classroom. Administrators in schools of education at colleges and universities need to develop and enforce policies/practices that address the assessment of set disposition criteria for teacher candidates. National and state accreditation bodies can assist schools of education by providing disposition statements as well as assessment models. Case law has demonstrated that the courts typically support the professional judgment of faculty and administrators in the use of disposition criteria

find that they are required to seek evidence of the Learner and Learning, Content Knowledge, Instructional Practice, and Professional Responsibility. While both knowledge and skills are viewed as measurable, institutions have struggled with a valid and reliable means to assess dispositions and ethical practices. This chapter reviews dispositional case law as it relates to professional preparation programs.

HISTORICAL INSTITUTIONAL RESPONSIBILITY

Although U.S. colleges of education claim the responsibility to evaluate the dispositions toward teaching held by students in their programs, the ultimate responsibility oftentimes falls on individual professors to assess student dispositions. While assessment of student knowledge and performance might be based on measurement through formal assessment instruments, such as tests, assessment of student disposition might be based on nonobjective measures, including informal observations and interactions. That is, the professor becomes the instrument to assess student fitness based on dispositions. Accordingly, critics of student dispositions as criteria for teacher candidacy question the resulting grade or evaluation because of its inherent subjectivity and seemingly value-laden judgments (Borko, Liston, & Whitcomb, 2007; Miller, Linn, & Gronland, 2009).

A professor generally determines whether and how well each student meets content and performance expectations. In assigning grades, a professor explicitly or implicitly endorses each candidate for certification on dispositional grounds as promoting the belief that "good" grades often imply that a candidate will be a "good" teacher. Value judgments are inherent in evaluation; however, there are distinct differences between the evaluation of student knowledge and skills and that of student dispositions (Diez, 2007).

First, knowledge and skills are measureable and observable, while dispositions, it has been argued, are not (Miller et al., 2009). While content and performance assessment is not a measure of inherent qualifications of an individual person, dispositional assessment, for some critics of teacher education, is viewed as specifically related to one's inherent qualification as a potential practitioner. Second, while formal assessment of the extent to which a teacher candidate demonstrates knowledge and skills acquired in the course of a teacher education program seems reasonable, it may be questionable to what extent, if any, a candidate's disposition is related to a particular course or program of study (Diez, 2007; Johnson, 2008). The concern that programs have traditionally raised focuses attention on the student's First Amendment right to freedom of speech. That is, the right of a candidate to hold and profess beliefs that are contrary to accepted professional practice are rights guaranteed by the First Amendment of the U.S. Constitution. However, the right to act on these beliefs is not necessarily constitutionally protected and is subject to reasonable professional oversight which, under current accreditation requirements, extends to programs that prepare professional practitioners. As Daniel, Gee, Sun, and Pauken (2012) observe, teacher candidate dispositions maybe classified as "merely reasonable academic standards to be accorded a measure of respect" (p. 656). For instance, a student-teacher may subscribe to religious beliefs that children who identify as gay, lesbian, bisexual, or transgender are manifesting sinful lives. That belief may fall under First Amendment protection, yet a student-teacher's conduct that demonstrates exclusion or other alienation is likely not protected under the First Amendment (cf. Head v. Board of Trustees, 2007).

Accreditation, under the Council for the Accreditation of Educator Preparation (CAEP) standards, is incumbent upon a program of professional preparation to assess and ensure that graduates will act in a manner commensurate with professional ethical expectations of the profession. In order to comply with those standards, programs intending to assess the dispositions of candidates need to shift their focus from beliefs, values, and attitudes to observable and measureable behaviors. For example, a candidate may believe that homosexuality is an abomination, but if that candidate is to teach in the public schools, then that candidate must be able to work effectively, ethically, and without bias with students and their families regardless of a students' or their families' sexual orientation. Thus, a candidate who articulates such beliefs in a teacher preparation class may raise concerns for the faculty member if the candidate does not appear able to resolve these beliefs in terms of conduct in a PK–12 classroom. This resolution suggests that there is a distinction in how one is evaluated between the beliefs and the overt behaviors, since it is the behaviors, and not the beliefs, that are required by the profession. Illustrative of this increased emphasis on understanding the value of inclusion is the current Dignity for All Students Act (DASA) in New York State as well as the new New York State *Educating All Students* test that all teacher education candidates must take and pass in order to be certified to teach in New York State. Nonetheless, the legal treatment of these dispositions to teacher preparation programs must be understood to contextualize how faculty in these programs might address challenges to student-teacher disposition standards.

LEGAL TRENDS IN DISPOSITIONAL EVALUATION

Recently, a shift has begun to occur as American courts have permitted challenges to institutional determination of academic qualification and demanded that procedural guidelines be implemented and enforced

(McConnell v. LeMoyne, 2006). This shift has occurred in many fields of professional practice, and teacher certification has not been spared. There has been a long-standing belief among educators that distinguishable qualities exist between capable teachers and individuals who are not well fit for the profession (Darling-Hammond, 1995, 2000; Ross & Bruce, 2007). What cannot be agreed upon, however, is how these qualities can be validly and reliably measured (Diez, 2007; Johnson, 2008). Similar to Justice Potter Stewart's inability to define "obscenity" in *Jacobellis v. Ohio* (1964) as "you know when you see it," some educators have reported that they know a poor candidate when they see one, but that identification schema does not articulate a measurable criteria. In the current litigious climate, dismissing a preservice candidate based on professional judgment deemed as "poor" dispositions without some form of objective evidence and without clearly defined due process procedures that must be followed will subject the institution to legal challenge that may well be successful in reinstating the student back into the preservice program (see McConnell v. LeMoyne, 2006).

While a shift in dispositional assessment is now occurring, the validity and reliability of such assessments are critical. As evidenced by the response received to the instrument created by Rinaldo, Denig, Sheeran, Vermette, and Smith (2009), there is a clear need for such assessments. Current initiatives in New York and other states to implement dispositional assessments by commercial enterprises have yet to produce verifiable data that validates the instrument's use for its intended purpose. Thus, a clear problem is the assessment instrument (Diez, 2007; Johnson, 2008).

REQUIRED ELEMENTS IN THE ASSESSMENT PROCESS

As scholars of teacher education have noted, one solution is that colleges of education must focus on the need to document and measure their effectiveness and their success (e.g., see Nelsen, 2015). While it has been a long-standing tradition of a school, college, or department of education (SCDE) to assess teacher candidate progress based on knowledge acquisition, educators over the past century have suggested that dispositions are an important component of demonstrated teacher competency and that there is a need to include them as part of the final evaluation (Dewey, 1007/1916; McNeil, 1971; Miller, 2000; Noddings, 2002; Palmer, 1983; van Manen, 1986). Although many educational leaders appear to agree that there is a need to address the whole individual, these qualities are not typically assessed with the same rigor as other teacher attributes (Balzano & Murray, 2003). Nonetheless, a dialogue on reframing these dispositions and consideration of their alignment with the law seem inevitable in the debate over how to address teacher candidate dispositions.

Whether qualitative or quantitative, whether measured or assessed, whether overt or implied, recognition of teacher candidate dispositions compose part of any teacher education program's efficacy Therefore, SCDEs are faced with three difficult tasks. They must (a) create operational definitions of dispositional qualities that they expect of their graduates, (b) develop an instrument which allows them to measure teacher candidate dispositions over the course of the program, and (c) create a process which provides intervention for candidates who fall short (Rinaldo, Denig, Sheeran, Cramer-Benjamin et al., 2009). Finally, there is a clear need to assess and evaluate whether or not candidates exemplify these qualities upon graduation.

Balzano and Murray (2003) have indicated that, "while dispositions are listed, discussed and even debated, they are not subject to the same rigor of assessment, if assessed at all" (p. 1). Few administrative evaluations place emphasis on the intangible aspects of teaching, choosing instead to accentuate the importance of clearly measurable and observable behaviors which can more easily be construed as self-evident. Nonetheless, intangible qualities such as curiosity, imagination, empathy, innovation, interest, and compassion play a significant role in student success and are therefore integrated into professional preparation programs (Miller, 2000; Palmer, 1983; van Manen, 1986). Thus, the dialogue should shift to examining measurable constructs that adhere to legal standards of reasonable professional standards as opposed to the current debate of seemingly arbitrary constructs within professional dispositions.

ACADEMIC FREEDOM AND THE RIGHTS OF A UNIVERSITY

There is some consensus among teachers and administrators concerning the tangible elements of good teaching (e.g., classroom management, planning and organization, the implementation of evidence-based instruction, and valid and reliable assessments of student progress) (Stronge, 2007). However, requirements for the intangible qualities are vague as defined by the National Council for Accreditation of Teacher Education (NCATE) Standard 1g:

> Candidates work with students, families, colleagues, and communities in ways that reflect the professional dispositions expected of professional educators as delineated in professional, state, and institutional standards. Candidates demonstrate classroom behaviors that create caring and supportive learning environments and encourage self-directed learning by all students. Candidates recognize when their own professional dispositions may need to be adjusted and are able to develop plans to do so. (NCATE, 2008; see also CAEP, n.d.)

to him by authorized representatives of it and was entitled to receive the degree" (p. 1). The result of these decisions was that material produced or published by colleges and universities was judicially construed as contractually binding and that if contractual conditions were met, there were contractual obligations that also must be met. "At both private and public institutions," note Professors Kaplin and Lee (2013), "the failure to follow institutional policies, rules, and regulations... led to successful litigation by students who claimed that their rights were violated by this noncompliance" (p. 840).

Since *Healy*, a number of lawsuits filed by students dismissed from professional certification programs have added a constitutional dimension to academic discipline. In *Stretten v. Wadsworth Veterans Hospital* (1976), the U.S. Court of Appeals for the Ninth Circuit found that Stretten had a property interest in retaining his medical school residency but disagreed on whether the deprivation of this right required a full-scale adversarial hearing consistent with the Fifth Amendment to the U.S. Constitution's due process requirements. It was clear, however, that admission to certain professional certification programs could be construed as a property interest subject to constitutional protection.

Only 2 years later, in *Missouri v. Horowitz* (1978), a student appealed her dismissal from medical school based on performance and dispositional assessments by faculty members. In addition to below-average achievement in her clinical placements and erratic attendance, faculty members found Horowitz, "lacked a critical concern for personal hygiene" (p. 7). She alleged the dismissal violated her Fourteenth Amendment rights. The Supreme Court of the United States cited its watershed 1974 decision in *Goss v. Lopez* (1975): "Whether to dismiss a student for academic reasons requires an expert evaluation of cumulative information and is not readily adapted to the procedural tools of judicial or administrative decision-making" (p. 594). In order for Horowitz to avail herself of Fourteenth Amendment protection, she had to establish that her enrollment in medical school constituted a property interest under state law. Even if the court were to assume a property interest, the Court opined that Horowitz had been given more than sufficient notice of poor assessments by faculty members in her program.

The U.S. Supreme Court affirmed the Horowitz decision 7 years later in *University of Michigan v. Ewing* (1985). Ewing sued the university after he was dismissed from a joint BA-MD program after failing a standardized test. He alleged his interest in continued enrollment required that the university satisfy substantive due process rights as required by the Fourteenth Amendment. Writing for a unanimous court, Justice John Paul Stevens found that academic decisions would have to depart substantially from accepted academic norms of professional judgment before the courts would intervene.

Then, 7 years later, in *Lunde v. Iowa Board of Regents* (1992), another student dismissed from a medical school on dispositional grounds challenged the decision under the Fourteenth Amendment. The faculty in that case had taken issue with Lunde for constantly sleeping in class and her antagonist relationship with her peers. Citing *Horowitz*, the Iowa court found that Lunde was afforded adequate due process protection. The court applied the reasoning in Horowitz, noting that Lunde's "ability to function in a clinical setting, including interaction with other health professionals, was an appropriate academic consideration" (p. 7). Thus, more explicitly than in the Supreme Court decision in Horowitz, the Iowa Court of Appeals affirmed and substantiated the use of dispositional criteria in addition to grades as "appropriate academic consideration(s)" (p. 6) in the dismissal of a preservice student from a professional certification program.

In *Van De Zilver v. Rutgers University* (1997), the U.S. District Court for New Jersey upheld the dismissal of a student from a medical degree program for "non-cognitive" (p. 4) reasons in addition to poor grades. Faculty members found Van De Zilver "had failed to demonstrate the maturity, dedication and nonacademic qualities expected of joint program participants" (p.7). He had consistently received poor grades, ignored advice to seek remedial instruction, and declined to take advantages of opportunities to increase his grades. Nonetheless, Van De Zilver alleged a number of due process and other constitutional violations. The U.S. District Court acknowledged that the "non-cognitive" factors were not easily discerned from the record but nonetheless refused to disturb the decision reached by the Rutgers administration. "After carefully reviewing the undisputed material facts of record in light of well-established legal precedent," wrote Justice Orlofsky, "I conclude that I cannot override the professional judgment of the faculty" (p. 4).

"Non-cognitive" or dispositional factors in academic disciplinary decisions were upheld by the U.S. Court of Appeals for the Eighth Circuit in *Richmond v. Fowlkes* (2000). Fowlkes was dismissed from a pharmaceutical program based on dispositional grounds, including lack of preparedness, tardiness, immaturity, and poor interpersonal relations. The Federal Court of Appeals substantiated and extended the position taken by the New Jersey District Court in *Van De Zilver* and affirmatively cited the U.S. Supreme Court in *Ewing*: "When judges are asked to review the substance of a genuinely academic decision, . . . they should show great respect for the faculty's professional judgment" (p. 6).

While these decisions suggest that enrollment in professional certification programs offered by private and public universities may give rise to a cognizable property interest such that academic sanctions, including dismissal, may attract constitutional scrutiny on due process grounds, it is abundantly clear that the courts have been unwilling to intervene in academic disciplinary decisions made by faculty and administrators in medical colleges.

In Mc*Connell v. LeMoyne College* (2006), McConnell was conditionally admitted to the graduate teacher education program at Le Moyne College, provided he successfully complete some prerequisite coursework. In one of these courses, McConnell expressed views in favor of corporal punishment and against multiculturalism. McConnell received an A– on the paper, but his expressed beliefs cast doubt in the minds of some faculty members on his suitability for the teaching profession. After he was dismissed from the program, McConnell filed suit. At trial, the lower court dismissed his complaint, but on appeal, the Fourth Department Appellate Division ordered LeMoyne to reinstate McConnell, citing its failure to follow its own published procedures. The judgment taken at the appellate level reversed the trial court's position. It should be noted that the reversal in this case was not made in deference to the previous cases as it was made on the basis of a failure to provide due process rather than the right of the institution to establish its own dispositional criteria. The reason that the initial judgment was overturned was not because LeMoyne College established dispositional criteria that the courts found unconstitutional but rather because they failed to follow their own policies with respect to the implementation of these criteria.

In *Thompson v. Southeastern Louisiana University*, an unreported civil action filed in the U.S. District Court for the Eastern District of Louisiana in 2005, the Court found Thompson's free exercise rights under the First Amendment had been violated when she was dismissed from a teacher education program after reporting that her cooperating teacher repeatedly engaged in prayer in the classroom. When she complained to her university supervisor, the supervisor attempted to engage her in prayer and informed her that she would have to repeat the placement or fail the program (see Wilkerson & Lang 2007). Thompson won the case. While most would agree this was the appropriate outcome, this case demonstrates that some judges are willing to review academic disciplinary decisions made by administrators and clearly question the validity of some university decisions.

Most recently, in a dispute involving Ed Swan, a 42-year-old conservative Christian enrolled in a teacher certification program at Washington State University, the Foundation for Individual Rights in Education (FIRE, 2005) wrote a letter to the university president arguing against the dispositional assessment criteria employed by the College of Education (see Wilkerson, 2007). One of the candidate dispositions assessed by faculty involved being "sensitive to community and cultural norms of the teacher education program, the university, and practicum settings." (p. 1). One professor expressed concern that,

> Mr. Swan has voiced some of his opinions, primarily though written papers, that I believe are in conflict with the program and department's cultural norms. Specifically, I am concerned about language that was expressed in one of his papers where he used the term "wetback" to describe recent Mexican immigrants. (FIRE, 2005b, para. 3)

The same professor also expressed serious consternation regarding Swan's views on race, gender, sexual orientation, and privilege. Apparently Swan had expressed his belief that "white privilege and male privilege [do] not exist," (para. 3), that homosexuality was wrong, and that a woman's place was in the home. Another professor gave Swan a negative dispositional score based on the fact that Swan had written "diversity is perversity" in a written assignment. Nonetheless, the first professor gave Swan an A in her course based on assessments of his content knowledge and performance. In her view, he was "an excellent student apart from his comments and choices" (FIRE, 2005a, para. 15).

In each of the last three cases reviewed, the courts intervened when teacher education programs appeared not to either clearly outline their criteria or follow their own procedures in removing students from preservice preparation programs. The rationale for removal was dispositional deficiencies; however, the basis of judgment used to effect the removals was more intuitive than factual. That is, professional judgment notwithstanding, the courts have remained consistent in that they require institutions to identify standards and procedures that must be adhered to in order to render a decision that is legally sufficient.

While there appears to be a disconnect between what courts have applied regarding the autonomy of the academy as it relates to the judgments of most professional programs and teacher education preservice programs, the solution appears quite obvious. Most professional programs, including law, medicine, dentistry, pharmacy, and the like, have highly designed and developed procedures and instruments that provide several objective measures of dispositional assessment; however, it appears that teacher preparation programs may be lacking in this regard. As the field of teacher preparation moves forward, greater attention must be paid to this critical aspect of preservice candidates' qualifications. To achieve these aims, evaluators must develop valid, reliable, and objective measures of dispositions, which are both clearly articulated and legally grounded. Only then will teacher preparation programs be on safe legal grounds to support decisions that will help to shape the landscape of the future of the profession.

Clearly these concerns are universal in nature. That is, appropriate dispositional orientation is both expected and demanded in the professional preparation of all practitioners. This is, however, particularly important as it relates to teacher candidates. Given that teachers are expected to appropriately educate all students who appear in their classrooms, teachers need

ABOUT THE CONTRIBUTORS

Christine Bellini, MEd, is a doctoral student in the department of Leadership Adult and Higher Education at the Ontario Institute for Studies in Education/University of Toronto. She is also a secondary school teacher with the Peel District School Board and an Instructor at the Faculty of Education at Lakehead University. Christine has been a Gay Straight Alliance Advisor for the past 8 years and is interested in teacher education, social justice, and student advocacy. She can be reached at christine.bellini@utoronto.ca.

Susan C. Bon, JD, PhD, is associate professor of education and law in the Department of Educational Leadership and Policies at the University of South Carolina. Her scholarship focuses on the impact of law and ethics on leadership and special education leadership in K–12 schools and higher education programs. She has published nearly 40 education law articles and book chapters, and is an active leader in national law-related organizations.

Christa Brodina, MEd, was born and raised in Bismarck, North Dakota. She attended the University of North Dakota double majoring in business and vocational education and marketing education and completed her master's in educational leadership. Currently she is the CTE Director at the Lake Area Career and Technology Center and Assistant Principal at Devils Lake High School in Devils Lake, North Dakota. Christa is married to Dustin, and they have four beautiful children, Beau, Parker, Tylie, and Benjamin.

Law and Education Inequality, pages 173–178

Gerald M. Cattaro, EdD, is professor and Executive Director of the Center for Catholic School Leadership and Faith Based Education in the Graduate School of Education at Fordham University in New York City. Before joining the faculty at Fordham, he was a principal for 18 years, a high school teacher, and junior high school teacher. Dr. Cattaro currently serves on several international and national governing boards, editorial boards, and educational commissions. He received his doctorate from Teachers College, Columbia University.

Philip T. K. Daniel, JD, EdD, is the William and Marie Flesher Professor of Educational Administration and Adjunct Professor of Law at The Ohio State University. He is a former President of the Education Law Association and served as a member of the ELA Board of Directors for several years. He is the author of numerous scholarly publications and is co-author of the books *Law and Public Education* (5th ed., 2014); *Law, Policy and Higher Education* (2012); and *Education Law and the Public Schools: A Compendium* (1998). His work is continually cited by researchers nationally and internationally and in legislation and the courts. He is a member of the Editorial Advisory Committee of West's Education Law Reporter and is on the editorial boards of the Brigham Young University *Journal of Education Law* and the *Journal of Education and Urban Society.*

Kent Divoll, EdD, is a tenured associate professor in the School of Education's Teacher Education Program at the University of Houston-Clear Lake (UHCL). Currently in his 7th year at UHCL, Dr. Divoll teaches undergraduate and master's courses in classroom management, curriculum, and instructional strategies; supervises graduate and undergraduate practicum students; and serves on dissertation committees. His research interests include classroom management, relational pedagogy, teacher preparation, and the scholarship of teaching and learning. He has served as the Chair, Vice Chair, and Program Chair for the American Education Research Association's (AERA) Classroom Management SIG. In addition, Dr. Divoll is the faculty advisor for the education honor society, Kappa Delta Pi, at UHCL.

Richard T. Geisel, JD, PhD, has a background in law, teaching, and curriculum leadership. He received his Juris Doctor in 1993, his Michigan teaching certificate in 1996, and his PhD in organizational leadership in 2002. Currently, he is associate professor in the Educational Leadership Department at Grand Valley State University in Grand Rapids, Michigan, and teaches primarily in the area of school law. Dr. Geisel's research interests include disability law, civil rights, parental rights, First Amendment law for students and public school employees, as well as issues surrounding the legal literacy of school administrators.

Bettye Grigsby, PhD, obtained her doctorate in curriculum and instruction with an emphasis on multicultural education at Texas A&M University in College Station, Texas. Dr. Grigsby had been a public school classroom teacher and served as an administrator on the secondary level for more than 18 years. Currently, she is associate professor at the University of Houston-Clear Lake in the area of educational administration and an educational consultant for Pre-K–12 schools, providing professional development to support them in improving instruction for all students. Dr. Grigsby has presented at national conferences and published articles on issues related to educational administration, principal preparation programs, hiring practices, and higher education.

Sonya Douglass Horsford, EdD, is associate professor of education in the Graduate School of Education and College of Education and Human Development at George Mason University. Her research interests include the political and policy contexts of education leadership with a focus on educational equality, opportunity, and reform in the post–Civil Rights Era.

Angie Jonasson, MEd, has worked in education for the last 18 years as a teacher, mentor, and now administrator. She is currently principal of West Elementary School in Grand Forks, North Dakota. Ms. Jonasson holds an MEd in educational leadership from the University of North Dakota in December of 2011.

Lawrence Kajs, EdD, is associate dean and professor in the School of Education at the University of Houston-Clear Lake (UHCL). He earned his doctoral degree in administration, planning, and social policy from Harvard University. His research has focused on administrative strategies that address a proactive approach for school and university improvement, particularly on the topic of legal issues. Dr. Kajs is a regular contributor to West's *Education Law Reporter.*

Brenda R. Kallio, EdD, spent the early part of her teaching career working with children with special needs. In 2000, she earned her doctorate from Bowling Green State University. Currently, she is professor at the University of North Dakota where she teaches courses in public school law and special-education law. Dr. Lallio's research interests include legal/ethical decision-making, at-risk students, the legal knowledge base of school administrators, and the First Amendment as it applies to teacher freedoms.

Daniel Kiel, JD, is associate professor at the University of Memphis Cecil C. Humphreys School of Law. In addition to his writing on race and education, which has appeared in a variety of law reviews and periodicals, he proposed and enacted legislation. Ms. Snyder lectures nationally and is a contributing author on various special-education law and education law topics. She is admitted to practice law before the U.S. District Court for the eastern, middle and western districts of Pennsylvania, the U.S. District Court for New Jersey, the Pennsylvania Supreme Court, the New Jersey Supreme Court, and the Ohio Supreme Court. She is a registered lobbyist in Pennsylvania. Ms. Snyder can be reached by telephone at (610) 524-8454 or by email at nsnyder@ldylaw.com

Jeffrey C. Sun, JD, PhD, is professor of higher education at the University of Louisville and a Visiting Scholar at The Ohio State University. He taught previously at NYU, Columbia, and North Dakota. He researches and writes in the area of higher-education law, and his teaching centers around law, policy, and organizational analyses. Dr. Sun also serves on the Board of Directors for the Association for the Study of Higher Education (ASHE) and the Executive Board of the Law & Education SIG of the American Educational Research Association (AERA). Dr. Sun received a BBA and MBA from Loyola Marymount University, a law degree from the Moritz College of Law at The Ohio State University, and an MPhil. and a PhD from Columbia University.